MONOGRAPHS OF THE
SOCIETY FOR RESEARCH IN
CHILD DEVELOPMENT

SERIAL NO. 224, VOL. 56, NO. 2, 1991

JUDGING SOCIAL ISSUES:
DIFFICULTIES, INCONSISTENCIES,
AND CONSISTENCIES

ELLIOT TURiEL
CAROLYN HILDEBRANDT
CECILIA WAINRYB

WITH COMMENTARY BY
HERBERT D. SALTZSTEIN

D1531644

MONOGRAPHS OF THE SOCIETY FOR RESEARCH IN CHILD
DEVELOPMENT, SERIAL NO. 224, VOL. 56, NO. 2, 1991

CONTENTS

ABSTRACT

TURIEL, ELLIOT; HILDEBRANDT, CAROLYN; and WAINRYB, CECILIA. Judging Social Issues: Difficulties, Inconsistencies, and Consistencies. With Commentary by HERBERT D. SALTZSTEIN. *Monographs of the Society for Research in Child Development*, 1991, **56**(2, Serial No. 224).

The three studies reported in this *Monograph* examine high school and college students' reasoning about the issues of abortion, homosexuality, pornography, and incest. The studies stemmed from previous research on reasoning in the "prototypical" moral, social conventional, and personal domains. We postulated that abortion, homosexuality, pornography, and incest are nonprototypical issues. We expected that reasoning about nonprototypical and prototypical issues would differ and that reasoning about nonprototypical issues would be inconsistent and involve ambiguities in informational assumptions.

Two groups were preselected in Study 1, those who negatively and those who positively evaluated the nonprototypical issues. Assessments were made of criterion judgments (evaluations, rule contingency, and generalizability) and justifications regarding moral, personal, and nonprototypical issues. The groups differed in judgments about the nonprototypical issues but not the moral issues. Both groups gave noncontingent and generalized judgments about moral issues, with justifications of justice and rights. Subjects who evaluated nonprototypical acts negatively used varied and often inconsistent configurations of criterion judgments. Responses coded for general reasoning types often entailed juxtapositions of prescriptive judgments and assertions of personal choice. Subjects who evaluated nonprototypical acts positively judged that they should be legal and nongeneralized and gave justifications based on personal choice.

Using similar procedures, Study 2 was conducted with practicing Catholics attending parochial high schools. The findings paralleled those of Study 1, including a split among subjects in their evaluations of the nonprototypical issues. The results suggested a bidirectional relation between individual judgments and group positions.

The findings of Studies 1 and 2 suggested that variations in evaluations and judgments about the nonprototypical issues were associated with variations in ambiguously held informational assumptions. Study 3 examined the role of such informational assumptions. It was found that assumptions associated with judgments about abortion and homosexuality were ambiguous and inconsistently applied. Thus, we propose that ambiguity around assumptions is a central component of the nonprototypicality of these issues.

I. INTRODUCTION

Consistencies and inconsistencies can be found both within and between individuals in their evaluations of important social issues. Whereas most people seem to agree that issues such as killing, theft, and rape are wrong, judgments about issues like abortion, homosexuality, and pornography are frequently marked by controversy and inconsistencies. Moreover, an individual will reason in different ways about different social actions, whether those actions are evaluated as right or as wrong. Thus, along with evaluations of the rightness or wrongness of an act, there are judgments as to whether it should be socially sanctioned or left to individual choice. There are also questions about whether social actions should be evaluated similarly across situations and contexts. An extensive series of studies (summarized in Smetana, 1983; Turiel, 1983; and Turiel, Killen, & Helwig, 1987) has led us to conclude that individuals' patterns of reasoning along these dimensions differ according to the nature of the issue to which the judgment is applied. To date, our work has centered on the characteristics of reasoning about issues in what we term the *moral, social conventional,* and *personal* domains. In this *Monograph,* we turn our attention to a set of complex and socially significant issues—abortion, homosexuality, pornography, and incest—issues that, we propose, do not fall unambiguously into any one of those three domains. We first briefly recapitulate the position advanced through previous research (which may be familiar to some readers) and then indicate what led us to hypothesize that the nature of the issues that we examine here would differ from that of those previously investigated.

DOMAINS OF SOCIAL REASONING

The postulation of domain distinctions is based on analytic distinctions drawn by philosophers (e.g., Dworkin, 1978; Gewirth, 1978; Rawls, 1971) between moral imperatives and the standards, conventions, or practices of social organizations and institutions. Within this framework, "morality" re-

1

fers to concepts of welfare, justice, and rights, and "social convention" refers to shared uniformities based on social organization. The distinction between convention and morality has been summarized by Turiel et al. (1987, pp. 169–170) as follows:

> Conventions are part of constitutive systems and are shared behaviors (uniformities, rules) whose meanings are defined by the constituted system in which they are embedded. Adherence to conventional acts is contingent on the force obtained from socially constructed and institutionally embedded meanings. Conventions are thus context-dependent and their content may vary by socially constructed meanings. While morality also applies to social systems, it is not constitutive or defined by existing social arrangements. In this perspective on morality, prescriptions are characterized as unconditionally obligatory, generalizable, and impersonal insofar as they stem from concepts of welfare, justice, and rights.

The personal domain comprises actions considered outside the jurisdiction of moral concern or social regulation and legitimately within the jurisdiction of personal choice.

Over 40 studies have been conducted on children's and adolescents' judgments in these domains (see Helwig, Tisak, & Turiel, 1990; and Turiel et al., 1987). Two dimensions of reasoning in each domain have been identified: criterion judgments and justifications. Assessments of criterion judgments are used to determine the characteristics by which individuals identify, define, and distinguish among the domains. These criterion judgments have included evaluations of the acts themselves (e.g., right or wrong, permissible or not), of rule or authority status and contingency (whether there should be a rule or law and whether the act would be right or wrong in the absence of a rule or law), of personal jurisdiction (whether the propriety of the act can be determined by personal choice or inclination), of consensus (whether the evaluation of the act should be determined by group agreement or cultural standards), and of religious practice (whether religious doctrine determines the evaluation of the act). In addition, assessments have been made of individuals' forms of reasoning or justifications in evaluations and judgments of social actions.

There is a large body of evidence demonstrating that individuals apply different criterion judgments to issues in the moral, social conventional, and personal domains. In studies of criterion judgments, individuals are typically presented with what we refer to as "prototypical" issues for each domain. In the case of prototypical moral issues (e.g., inflicting physical harm on others, theft, unequal distribution, and discrimination), the research has documented that children and adolescents identify and define morality

2

through the criteria of obligatoriness, nonalterability, and generalizability. Moral prescriptions are judged to be obligatory, not subject to arbitrary change, not contingent on existing rules or laws, not dependent on authority dictates, and applicable across situations and social contexts. Moreover, moral judgments are structured by concepts of justice, rights, and welfare—as evinced by individuals' justifications for their evaluations of moral issues. Moral judgments, therefore, entail concerns with the welfare of others, just or fair resolutions of competing claims among people, and the maintenance of rights. Judgments in the moral realm are not contingent on rules or authority, nor are they conceived to be directly tied to existing social arrangements.

A contrasting pattern of judgments is associated with social conventions (examples of prototypical items are forms of address, modes of dress, and forms of greeting). Conventions are regarded as tied to aspects of the social context and, therefore, judged to be contingent on rules, authority, and existing social practice. As part of the social or cultural context, conventions are judged to be nongeneralizable and relative to social systems. Justifications of conventional regularities evince that conventions are structured by concepts of social organization, including authority, custom, and social coordination.

Additionally, it has been found that children and adolescents regard a set of nonmoral actions as within the jurisdiction of personal choice (Nucci, 1981; Smetana, 1988; Stoddart & Turiel, 1985). Personal issues are judged to be areas of individual prerogative that apply mainly to the self (e.g., issues of privacy, actions judged to be harmless to others). Insofar as nonmoral actions are not part of the conventionally regulated system, they are judged to be within the personal realm. It has been found, moreover, that certain actions (e.g., use of some types of drugs) are regarded by some persons as matters of personal discretion and, therefore, illegitimately regulated by convention (Berkowitz, Guerra, & Nucci, in press).

There is substantial evidence indicating that, starting in early childhood, differentiations are made among moral, conventional, and personal concepts. These differentiations, however, are made in less consistent and comprehensive ways by younger children (approximately 4–8 years) than by older children and adolescents (Turiel, 1989a). Moreover, age-related changes were found in forms of reasoning within the domains. For example, younger children's justifications for moral evaluations are characterized primarily by concerns with avoiding harm to others and promoting welfare, whereas older children also account for reciprocity with justifications pertaining to fairness and justice (Davidson, Turiel, & Black, 1983). A sequence of developmental levels and transitions has also been identified for understandings of social convention (for details, see Turiel, 1983, chap. 6).

Our proposition of domain specificity stands in contrast with "global" approaches, which would encompass the various issues we differentiate by domain into the moral realm and its development. One global approach (e.g., Kohlberg, 1969; Piaget, 1932) characterizes moral development as a series of progressive differentiations among what we distinguish as domains. A central component in this approach is the proposition that, with age, children come to distinguish convention from morality, subordinating the former to the latter. In another global approach (e.g., Shweder, 1986; Shweder, Mahapatra, & Miller, 1987), it is proposed that the individual's moral evaluations and judgments are determined primarily by central and homogeneous moral orientations that can be identified at the cultural level. Insofar as individuals distinguish between domains, it is as a consequence of a cultural orientation to morality that includes personal choice and in which some norms can be treated as alterable and contingent (e.g., societies with moral ideologies emphasizing individual autonomy). It is proposed that, in cultures structured by social hierarchy and concomitant duties, all social practices are treated as morally fixed and obligatory. Specifically relevant to the present research is the fact that these two types of global approaches would, each in its own way, treat all social issues as unambiguously part of the moral realm. For instance, within the model of progressive differentiations, issues like pornography and abortion have been examined solely from the perspective of a sequence of moral judgments (Gilligan, 1977; Gilligan, Kohlberg, Lerner, & Belenky, 1970). Within the cultural orientation model, abortion, pornography, homosexuality, and incest are quintessential moral issues insofar as their immorality is strongly sanctioned by society.

Issues and domains.—As noted earlier, a hypothesis guiding the present research is that issues such as abortion, homosexuality, incest, and pornography do not clearly fall into the moral domain. Before presenting the rationale for this hypothesis, it would be useful to make brief mention of how we construe the relation between issues and domains of reasoning. This is a complex problem addressed elsewhere (see esp. Turiel & Davidson, 1986; and Turiel et al., 1987), and we can provide only the outlines here. We do wish to stress, however, the importance of categorizing the nature of issues or events presented to research subjects in order to maximize their likelihood of correspondence with the domain under study (for detailed discussions, see Turiel, 1978; and Turiel et al., 1987). Our strategy has been to use the definitions of the domains to guide the categorizations of issues and then to test those categorizations by examining the ways in which subjects reason about the given issue. The body of findings has led us to the conclusion that issues cannot be classified wholly independently of how they are construed by individuals and that how individuals reason about issues is not independent of features of the issue.

This is an interactive and interpretive position in that the elements of issues or events are not in an arbitrary relation with individuals' domains of judgment. That is, features of events are processed and interpreted by individuals from the perspective of their own domain-differentiated judgments. For instance, the prototypical moral issues used in our research, such as inflicting harm on others, theft, or unequal distribution, contain features that bear on persons' moral reasoning. These are intentional (i.e., not accidental) acts with negative consequences for others (e.g., physical or psychological harm, injustice), and the victim is an unwilling participant. Given that moral judgments are characterized by noncontingency and generalizability, prototypical moral issues are not context dependent in the same ways as conventional and personal issues.[1] Conventions do not have features like intentional harm or injustice; they are behavioral uniformities that function within a network of shared meaning. Conventions are relative and context dependent insofar as the functions they serve vary across groups and alternative ones can serve the same functions. Consequently, issues or events can be part of conventional regulation in one context and not in another, where they might be left to personal jurisdiction.

We can illustrate the context dependency of issues concretely with reference to the procedures and findings of a study by Miller and Bersoff (1988). In addition to including domain distinctions, Miller and Bersoff introduced a distinction between rules having high and low social utility (i.e., rules that involve efficiency and serve the general public interest and rules that are not instrumental in the attainment of common goals) and set those rules in public or private contexts. Children (7 and 11 years old) and adults were presented with incidents pertaining to (a) moral rules (not to kick others; not to take others' money), (b) nonmoral rules with high social utility (use green door to exit theater; stand in line at left to buy over 12 groceries), and (c) nonmoral rules with low social utility (say hello on meeting others; use silverware to eat foods like spaghetti; women students wear dresses to college speeches). Each incident was presented in a public or a private context; for example, the rule not to kick others was presented in the context of either a public park or a private health club, the rule to use a green door to exit a theater in the context of either a city fair or a private country club fair, and the rule that women wear dresses to public lectures in the context of either a state college or a private college.

The results showed unequivocally that, at all ages, evaluations, judgments, and justifications of the moral issues were not contingent on context. Whether set in public or private contexts, children and adults evaluated the

---

[1] The total situation must be considered even in the classification of acts in the moral domain (Turiel et al., 1987). For instance, one person thrusting a knife into another would in many circumstances be a clear example of a moral issue. If, however, the context is that of a surgeon operating on a patient to ensure his well-being, then the act takes on a different meaning by virtue of the actor's intentions and goals.

rules positively and transgressions of the rules negatively. They also judged that the acts in this domain should not be under personal jurisdiction and rejected the acceptability of altering the rules (to ones permitting kicking others and taking others' money). By contrast, nonmoral rules were context sensitive and judged by conventional criteria in some conditions and by personal criteria in others. Rules of high social utility were evaluated positively (in public and private contexts), and, in turn, transgressions were evaluated negatively. Whereas the majority of subjects judged that acts pertaining to high-social-utility rules should not be under personal jurisdiction, the majority also judged that it is acceptable to alter the rules (e.g., to use a red door to exit a theater) in either public or private contexts. Thus, subjects at all ages judged these rules by conventional criteria.

A different pattern of responses emerged for the low-social-utility rules, where some age-related findings were obtained. The large majority of subjects judged actions governed by these rules to be legitimately under personal jurisdiction and considered their transgression acceptable. However, low-social-utility rules were treated differently in public and private contexts by all but the youngest subjects. Consistent with the judgment that the acts are under personal jurisdiction, the majority in each age group rejected the legitimacy of this type of rule in public settings, in either its original form (e.g., women students wear dresses to college lectures) or an alternative form (e.g., women students wear pants to college lectures). The majority of the 7-year-olds also rejected the legitimacy of either form of low-social-utility rule in private contexts. By contrast, the majority of the 11-year-olds and adults did accept either form of low-social-utility rule in private settings. The findings with older subjects illustrate the contextual features of issues judged to be in the conventional and personal domains. For private settings, it was judged that restricted groups can legitimately institute rules governing behavior that in other contexts should remain under personal jurisdiction.

This age-related pattern of findings is consistent with the proposition that young children distinguish among the domains, but in less comprehensive ways than older children and adults. It is not consistent with the model of progressive age-related differentiations between domains because, at all ages, judgments about the moral rules differed from judgments applied to high-social-utility nonmoral rules, which in turn differed from judgments of personal jurisdiction applied to low-social-utility rules. Miller and Bersoff's findings also contradict the proposition (see esp. Gabennesch, 1990) that young children "reify" social practices and rules by perceiving them as fixed, unalterable, and everlasting natural entities (as opposed to human inventions). Not only did the youngest children clearly show distinct conceptions of the unalterable (for moral reasons of avoiding harm and unfairness) and the alterable and contextual (by conventional criteria), but a majority of them also considered personal choice to override conventional regulations even in restricted private social contexts. This latter judgment reflects a detachment from certain social rules that contradicts the characterization of young children as mystifying or reifying social rules (for a more general discussion of evidence on this issue, see Helwig et al., 1990). Moreover, the overall findings of domain distinctions, along with the flexibility in applying judgments of convention and personal jurisdiction, suggest that individuals do not form a culturally determined homogeneous orientation.

DOMAIN DEMARCATIONS AND OVERLAP

The research demonstrating that children form distinct, organized systems of thought demarcated by domain is based on the use of what we label "prototypical issues" as stimuli to elicit subjects' judgments. In the moral domain, prototypical stimuli essentially present actions entailing harm, unfairness, or violations of rights in the absence of strong conflicting concerns. In the conventional domain, similarly, prototypical stimuli entail social organizational considerations that are not in conflict with moral or other social considerations. In proposing domain specificity, it is also necessary to consider how individuals make judgments about events that include components from more than one domain (which we refer to as "mixed domain events") as well as events that are not prototypical (Turiel & Davidson, 1986; Turiel & Smetana, 1984). It is plausible to hypothesize either that domains are entirely segregated categories or that there may be coordination between them. With regard to the latter hypothesis, we note that the possibility that individuals' judgments regarding multifaceted events combine or coordinate domains is neither logically nor psychologically inconsistent with the proposition of domain specificity. Category distinctions (as in the case of differentiating domains) do not logically imply that there can be no mixture or overlap between the categories (cf. Chomsky, 1980; Searle, 1983). According to Chomsky (1980, pp. 137–138), for instance, there can be situations involving relations between categories (e.g., between language and cognitive structures) even though there are properties specific to each category (e.g., properties of language-specific and cognition-specific structures). In a similar vein, Searle (1983) maintains that category distinctions do not preclude events or judgments that do not clearly fit the categories: "A distinction is no less a distinction for allowing a family of related, marginal, diverging cases" (p. 79).

The extent to which judgments are hypothesized to cross domain boundaries does depend on the psychological mechanisms proposed for the origins and application of judgments. For instance, explanations of domains as innately determined (e.g., Fodor, 1983) may include the proposition that

7

they have rigid demarcations. That is, it could be proposed that the innate mechanisms include impermeable domain boundaries. Our position, in contrast to the innate hypothesis, is that social judgments arise out of children's social experiences and entail conceptual transformations of social events (for details, see Turiel & Davidson, 1986; and Turiel et al., 1987). For the present purposes, the relevant feature of this position is that individuals interpret social events and thereby apply particular types (domains) of judgments. Situations with components from more than one domain would pose the conceptual task of coordinating or relating different types of judgments with each other.

Previous research has examined reasoning about multifaceted situations by presenting subjects with situations entailing conflicts between moral and conventional considerations. As examples, assessments were made both of children's judgments regarding conflicts between considerations of harm or fairness and classroom social organizational goals (Duncan, 1986; Killen, 1990) and of adolescents' judgments of conflicts between fairness and the structure of social organization in the family (Turiel, 1983, chap. 6). When addressing such multifaceted situations, children and adolescents attempted to interrelate or coordinate them in some fashion, in the context of having judged each component by domain-consistent criteria. The coordination strategies included explicitly giving priority to one over the other, reconciling the two through compromise solutions, or explicitly maintaining that the conflict cannot be reconciled in a satisfactory way. These strategies show that individuals account for the mixture of domains and do not simply segregate them. (For other aspects of mixed-domain judgments, see Jancaterino, 1982; and Stoddart & Turiel, 1985).

The focus of the present research was not on situations with a clear conflict between domains but on judgments about issues that may constitute "diverging cases," to use Searle's terminology. In the terminology to be used here, issues like abortion, homosexuality, pornography, and incest may be "nonprototypical" relative to the prototypical domains of the moral, conventional, and personal. The ways in which issues are nonprototypical with regard to the application of delineated categories require clarification and research into how individuals conceptualize them. Some initial indications that these issues can be appropriately classified as nonprototypical are derived from public discourse, especially in U.S. Supreme Court decisions and the results of public opinion surveys. Clearly, in the United States, these issues are intensely debated, and many of these debates go beyond polite discussion, sometimes even resulting in violence. The controversies revolve primarily around disagreements about the moral implications of these issues, about their cultural and legal status, and about basic assumptions regarding biological and psychological explanation. In addition to these controversies and central to the classification of the issues involved as nonprototypical is the fact that (*a*) the application of evaluative criteria is inconsistent and (*b*) differences exist in people's perceptions concerning the nature of these actions and their consequences.

PUBLIC DISCOURSE AND OPINION

The constitutional standing of abortion, homosexuality, and pornography is still very much in question. Recent Supreme Court rulings underscore and illustrate some of the central considerations entailed in positions taken on these issues. For example, the Court recently upheld the constitutionality of a Georgia statute forbidding private, consensual acts of homosexuality even in the privacy of one's own home (*Bowers v. Hardwick*, 1986). In the opinions supporting the majority (in a five to four margin), it was argued both that the Constitution does not grant individuals a fundamental right to engage in homosexual acts and that such prohibitions are rooted in history and tradition. In his supporting opinion, Chief Justice Burger stated, "Decisions of individuals relating to homosexual conduct have been subject to state intervention throughout the history of Western Civilization. Condemnation of these practices is firmly rooted in Judaeo-Christian moral and ethical standards. . . . To hold that the act of homosexual sodomy is somehow protected as a fundamental right would be to cast aside millennia of moral teaching."

In contrast, the minority view was that private, consensual sexual activity is a right protected by the Constitution. In his dissenting opinion, Justice Blackmun took issue with the proposition that constitutional questions can be decided by history or tradition: "It is precisely because the issue raised by this case touches the heart of what makes individuals what they are that we should be especially sensitive to the rights of those whose choices upset the majority. . . . That certain, but by no means all, religious groups condemn the behavior at issue gives the State no license to impose their judgments on the entire citizenry." It was further argued that homosexual activity is protected by the fundamental right of individuals to choose how to conduct intimate relations with others as long as they do not interfere with the rights of others.

The Supreme Court has also upheld federal and state regulations barring the sale of pornographic materials (*Roth v. United States*, 1957). The arguments revolved around freedom of expression, upholding community standards, and incitement of antisocial or criminal acts. The majority held that obscenity should not be protected as freedom of speech or of the press because it is "without redeeming social importance," it can incite antisocial behavior, and it can violate the standards of a community.

In *Roe v. Wade* (1973), a majority (seven to two) ruled that there is a constitutional right to privacy in a woman's decision to have an abortion. In that case, the arguments were over rights, protection of life, and potential harm to the mother or baby. It was ruled that statutes prohibiting abortion violate the Fourteenth Amendment on the grounds "that the right to personal privacy includes the abortion decision" as well as "that the word 'person' as used in the Fourteenth Amendment does not include the unborn." However, it was also maintained that "the right is not unqualified and must be considered against important state interests in regulation." .

The question of when life begins was considered central to the determination of how the woman's right to personal privacy is to be applied in cases regarding the termination of a pregnancy. However, instead of attempting to define when life begins—a question that was judged to be ambiguous and contested—the Court based its decision on the ability of the fetus to survive outside the womb. Prior to viability, the woman's decision is protected by the right to privacy: no restrictions can be placed on abortion during the first trimester of pregnancy; and, although states can regulate some medical aspects of abortion during the second trimester, they cannot prevent the procedure itself. During the third trimester—that is, after viability—states can impose restrictions on a woman's right to an abortion.

Constitutional rulings regarding abortion—as well as homosexuality and pornography—are far from settled (Tribe, 1990). There is a possibility, for instance, that *Roe v. Wade* will be reconsidered. Recently, by a five to four decision, the Supreme Court upheld some of Missouri's state regulations regarding abortion (*Webster v. Reproductive Health Services,* 1989). Myriad national surveys show that, among the general public, thinking about these issues is still in flux. More important, these survey data show a fair degree of inconsistency in most individuals' attitudes. First consider surveys assessing respondents' evaluations of actions and labeling of the "moral status" of pornography, abortion, and homosexuality. In surveys taken in 1977 and 1978 (*Time*/Yankelovich, Skelly, & White, as reported in McClosky & Brill, 1983), the majority of respondents considered pornography (in movies) (67%), abortion (57%), and homosexuality (58%) morally wrong.

However, regardless of "moral status," most people believe that abortion and homosexuality should not be prohibited by law. In a national opinion survey taken in 1978 (Harris & Westin, 1979), a representative cross section of adults was asked whether each of certain acts ought to be left to the discretion of an individual, allowed but regulated by law, or forbidden by law altogether. A majority (59%) stated that abortion should be a matter of individual discretion; 17% felt that it should be regulated by law, 21% that it should be totally forbidden by law. (In other surveys, majorities have stated that every woman wanting to have an abortion should be able to have one and that the decision to have an abortion during the early weeks of pregnancy should be left entirely to the woman.) A majority (70%) also stated that homosexuality (i.e., homosexual relations in private between consenting adults) should be a matter of individual discretion; 5% felt that it should be regulated by law, 20% that it should be totally forbidden by law.

However, a somewhat different pattern of attitudes emerged regarding pornography (i.e., selling pornographic magazines and films in bookstores): 17% stated that it should be left to the discretion of an individual, 30% that it should be regulated, and 44% that it should be totally forbidden. These results are consistent with other surveys (McClosky & Brill, 1983) showing that pluralities and majorities view pornography as harmful to community standards and believe that it ought to be regulated by law. Large proportions of respondents advocated censoring obscene books and pornographic films (to protect community standards), banning novels with explicit sex acts from high school libraries, and prohibiting the screening or airing of movies or television programs containing nudity and sex acts.

The variability in attitudes toward abortion and homosexuality is even more striking when surveys inquire into specific circumstances. For instance, a recent Gallup Poll (1988; see *New York Times*, January 22, 1989) showed that 24% of those sampled thought that abortion should be legal under any circumstances, 57% that it should be legal only under certain circumstances, and 17% that it should always be illegal (these results were consistent with a series of Gallup Poll results dating back to 1975; again, see *New York Times*, January 22, 1989). Abortion was considered appropriate action to take when a woman's life is endangered (94%), when a woman's health may be impaired (84%), when the pregnancy results from rape or incest (85%), and when the baby may be deformed (60%). In contrast, most people (75%) disapproved of abortion if performed because the family cannot financially afford to have the child.

Inconsistencies in attitudes toward homosexuality are demonstrated in responses to surveys of civil liberties (McClosky & Brill, 1983). As already mentioned, most people believe that homosexual relations should be a matter of individual discretion and not prohibited by law. At the same time, however, pluralities and majorities believe that there should be laws restricting particular liberties of homosexual groups and individuals. Approximately 50% of those sampled did not believe that homosexuals should have completely equal access to teaching and other public service positions and would endorse laws prohibiting bars for homosexuals. A majority believed that the community should not allow gay liberation movements to use a civic auditorium to promote homosexual rights (the right to assembly). Many people would also place legal prohibitions on marriage between homosexuals (59%) and on lesbian mothers' custody of their children (34% would not permit it, 32% would allow it, and the rest are undecided). McClosky and

Brill's survey also revealed negative attitudes toward homosexuals in that many viewed them as "sick and in need of help" and regarded gay liberation groups as being harmful to the country.

INCONSISTENCIES IN REASONING ABOUT NONPROTOTYPICAL ISSUES

There are correspondences between several elements of evaluation and judgment assessed in research on domains of social reasoning and those raised in the Supreme Court decisions and public opinion surveys just reviewed. These common elements include considerations of welfare, rights, legal status, community standards, individual prerogative, consensus, and religious doctrines. However, the survey data show patterns of evaluations of the nonprototypical issues that are not applied in judgments about the prototypical issues. Abortion, homosexuality, and pornography are evaluated by the majority of people as morally wrong, but the same people also believe that these acts should not be regulated by laws and that they should remain matters of personal choice. Such patterns differ from the typical constellation of within-individual judgments regarding prototypical moral issues. Most people believe that acts such as killing, assault, and theft are wrong and that they should be regulated by laws and subject to sanctions. Hence, individuals link their moral evaluations and judgments of legality to the judgment that the acts are not within the realm of personal jurisdiction (it is not typically stated that killing or stealing should be left to the individual's discretion).

Some of the concerns evident in public discussions and Supreme Court opinions illustrate ambiguities in the definitions of abortion, pornography, and homosexuality. In particular, disputes and ambiguities exist as to whether these acts entail harmful consequences. According to some, abortion is harmful because it involves the taking of a life. For others, it does not constitute harm because the fetus is not defined as constituting a human life. For many people, the definition of life and the determination of its beginning are ambiguous concepts that are difficult to specify.

The consequences of pornography are also in dispute. Some believe that pornography often leads to violent and criminal behavior, while others believe that it has no causal connection to violence, that it is objectionable merely as a breach of local community standards. Furthermore, it is often difficult to draw and justify the distinction between sexually obscene material of no socially redeeming value and sexual content in art or literature.

Disagreements regarding potential harmful consequences of homosexual behavior are also revealed by the surveys; some people view it as having negative effects on society, while others do not. In addition, ambiguities exist in judgments as to whether homosexuality constitutes some psychological or biological abnormality. On the one hand, the majority state that engaging in homosexual activity should be a matter of individual choice; on the other hand, however, the majority also want to impose legal restrictions on homosexuals' freedom of recreational choices (e.g., homosexual bars) and rights to assembly and marriage.

There is a fair amount of evidence, therefore, to suggest that judgments about these types of issues do not have the kind of coherence or organization that has been established to characterize judgments about a number of moral and conventional issues. However, the survey data are limited with regard to assessing how individuals make judgments about these issues because surveys only assess attitudes (respondents are typically asked to endorse one of two or three statements presented to them); they do not delve into associated conceptions. For instance, the finding that the majority of respondents evaluated abortion, homosexuality, and pornography as morally wrong could actually reflect differing conceptions of these actions as well as of the term "moral" itself. Moreover, the survey items and questions used were not based on a coherent set of criteria formulated in accord with social categories hypothesized to be relevant to the issues in question (e.g., definitions of domains of judgment).

Further research is needed into conceptions (e.g., criterion judgments and justifications) underlying attitudes expressed by survey respondents. Some information about judgmental criteria as applied to abortion is available from Smetana's (1982) research. Her study included judgments and justifications from several groups of subjects: pregnant women who had been referred to family-planning agencies; women from the same agencies who had never been pregnant; and male and (nonpregnant) female junior high and high school students. Responses to a semistructured interview about abortion, which included questions about the subject's own decision (for pregnant females) or a hypothetical situation (for males and nonpregnant females), showed that there is a fundamental distinction in the ways in which individuals conceptualize the status of the fetus as life and that this is associated with their evaluations of abortion. In all groups of subjects (pregnant and nonpregnant; females and males), individuals evaluating abortion as wrong believed that life begins at conception. Many of those evaluating abortion as permissible believed that life begins close to or at birth. In turn, some subjects placed the origins of life at an earlier phase of pregnancy, and some were ambivalent and undecided. These definitions of the unborn child were highly predictive of the pregnant women's subsequent decisions to terminate or continue their pregnancies.

In Smetana's study, assessments were also made of the application of the criterion of rule contingency to abortion in each trimester (i.e., the act is wrong even if there is no law; it is wrong only if there is a law) as well as to several prototypical moral acts. The results were consistent with those of

13

other studies. The large majority of subjects judged the prototypical moral issues wrong even in the absence of a law. In contrast, a large majority (90%) of the same subjects thought that there should be no law prohibiting abortion in the first trimester. Decreasing majorities thought that there should not be a law in the second (73%) and third (56%) trimesters. It was primarily those attributing life to the unborn who thought that abortion was wrong in the last two trimesters even in the absence of a law.

Smetana's findings illustrate the relevance of conceptions underlying attitudes to an understanding of an issue like abortion. In particular, the results point to the ways that premises about the origin of life can serve to produce different evaluations of an action. The findings also indicate that there is greater variability both between and within individuals' judgments regarding this nonprototypical issue than there is regarding prototypical issues.

THE CURRENT STUDIES

The three studies reported in this *Monograph* were aimed at ascertaining how adolescents and young adults make judgments about abortion, homosexuality, pornography, and incest. Note that no survey research has examined evaluations of incest; thus, we make no assumptions as to whether there is variation or consensus concerning this issue. Incest was included because it is governed by a strong cultural taboo, yet, if it occurs among consenting adults, its harmful consequences are ambiguous. A central aim of the research was to extend the work on domains of social reasoning to social topics that may not correspond clearly to domain distinctions documented by previous research. This would serve to include additional components of individuals' social judgments and to ascertain possible ambiguities in the demarcation of domains. The study included adolescents and young adults but not younger children because our aim was to delineate reasoning and potential inconsistencies in their more developed forms. Accordingly, we did not investigate the origins or developmental course of reasoning about these nonprototypical issues.

The present studies extend previous research in several ways. First, four nonprototypical issues were investigated and compared to prototypical ones. Second, a theoretically formulated set of criterion judgments was assessed, along with comprehensive analyses of reasoning through assessments of justification categories. Third, comparisons were made between groups of individuals who provided different evaluations of these issues. In Study 1, assessments of criterion judgments and justifications were made of groups of subjects who evaluated nonprototypical issues as morally wrong or as not morally wrong. Comparisons were also made between their judgments about the nonprototypical issues and their judgments about the prototypical moral and personal domains.

Subjects in Study 1 were randomly selected from two public high schools and a university, without any information regarding religious affiliation or degree of religiosity. Since religious doctrine often includes strict positions on the nonprototypical issues, it may be that the judgments of individuals with strong religious affiliations differ significantly from those of others. In Study 2, therefore, we investigated the criterion judgments and justifications of religious adolescents from a parochial high school. A final extension of previous research was guided by findings from Studies 1 and 2. In Study 3, a set of specific types of inconsistencies and contradictions (detailed in subsequent sections) in subjects' thinking about these issues was identified for further investigation.

II. STUDY 1: INCONSISTENCY
AND HETEROGENEITY IN SOCIAL REASONING

As we noted earlier, survey research indicates that people hold sharply divergent views regarding abortion, homosexuality, and pornography. Whereas some people evaluate these actions as morally wrong, others see them as acceptable and outside the moral realm. It also appears that judgments about these nonprototypical issues lack the coherence found to characterize judgments concerning prototypical moral and conventional issues. However, without study of the conceptions that underlie differing attitudes, such findings are inconclusive and could be misleading. To understand how individuals reason about these issues and apply different criterion judgments, it is necessary to investigate how they conceptualize the given act.

Study 1 was designed to generate such data by (*a*) examining individuals' criterion judgments and justifications of nonprototypical issues, (*b*) comparing the reasoning of those who evaluated them as wrong with the reasoning of those who saw them as acceptable, and (*c*) comparing reasoning about the nonprototypical and the prototypical moral and conventional-personal issues. To accomplish these goals, the study included subjects who evaluated nonprototypical issues as wrong (Group 1) and subjects who evaluated them as acceptable (Group 2), and it also assessed those subjects' reasoning about prototypical moral and conventional-personal issues.

To simplify our terminology in reporting the methods and results of the study, from here on the prototypical moral issues are referred to as "moral" and the prototypical conventional-personal ones as "personal." The nonprototypical issues continue to be labeled as such. We note one other simplification of terminology: the moral, personal, and nonprototypical categories will henceforth be referred to as "issue types."

SELECTION OF SUBJECTS

To facilitate the identification of subjects in filling the cells of the design, we used a preselection measure. This measure, however, provided only a tentative assignment of subjects to groups and issues. As explained below, the final assignments were based on a more extensive and therefore more reliable assessment of the subjects' evaluations of the acts.

The preselection measure was used to identify individuals who labeled any one exemplar of a set of nonprototypical issues as being a moral issue and evaluated it "not all right" or "depends" (Group 1) versus those who evaluated some such exemplar as both nonmoral and "all right" or "depends" (Group 2). Through the preselection measure, we also identified, for subjects in both groups, moral issues evaluated as wrong and personal issues viewed as acceptable.

The preselection measure was given to a pool of prospective subjects drawn from two high schools and a university in the San Francisco Bay Area (a total of 100 high school seniors and 122 undergraduates obtained from the subject pool of introductory psychology classes). Subjects were of various ethnic backgrounds; all came from families of middle-class socioeconomic status. The subjects were presented with a listing (in random order) of five nonprototypical issues (abortion, homosexuality, pornography, incest, and premarital sex), three moral issues (killing, rape, and theft), and four personal issues (nudity at a public beach, smoking marijuana, eating horse meat, and men wearing makeup) and asked to indicate in each instance whether the issue is "all right," "not all right," or "depends" as well as to judge whether it is a "moral issue." Examination of the pattern of responses on this measure led us to select four of the nonprototypical issues (abortion, homosexuality, pornography, and incest), two of the moral issues (killing and rape), and three of the personal ones (nudity, marijuana, and makeup) for further study. These particular issues were selected so as to have the largest number of subjects meeting the criteria for Groups 1 and 2.

Sample.—All prospective subjects qualified for inclusion in one of the two groups by the criteria noted above; selection of individuals for further study was made solely to achieve some balance in numbers of subjects involved to investigate the various issues in greater detail. All subjects contacted for this purpose agreed to participate in the study. The final sample included 87 high school seniors (45 males and 42 females, mean age 17-3) and 98 college undergraduates (54 males and 44 females, mean age 20-11). It should be stressed that, in the study itself, each subject was presented with only one nonprototypical, one moral, and one personal issue.[2] In all,

[2] While each subject was presented with only one nonprototypical issue, frequencies of responses on the preselection measure did show that Group 1 subjects generally responded to all four nonprototypical issues differently than Group 2 subjects did. Among Group 1 subjects, 53% evaluated all four issues as "wrong" or "depends"; 32% evaluated three and 14% two issues in that way. Among Group 2 subjects, 24% evaluated all four issues as "depends" or "wrong"; positive evaluations were given to one issue by 35%, to two issues by 31%, and to three issues by 11%.

however, four nonprototypical, two moral, and three personal issues were represented in the study. Table 1 shows the distribution by group, sex, and age of subjects administered the assessments of criterion judgments and justifications (as described below) for each issue.

Outcomes of the preselection measure.—In Table 2, we present the percentages of differing evaluations of the preselection items given by subjects in the final sample. Table 2 shows that the large majority of subjects evaluated the moral issues negatively and that they were divided in their evaluations of the personal issues. Subjects were also divided in their evaluations of all the nonprototypical issues, with the exception of incest, which the majority evaluated negatively. Table 2 also indicates that personal and nonprototypical issues were evaluated positively by more college than high school age subjects (significant differences, at $p < .05$ by chi-square tests, were found in evaluations of makeup, horse meat, and homosexuality).

Responses to the preselection measure also revealed that subjects' labeling of an issue as moral or nonmoral is of limited utility in predicting its evaluation and corresponding conceptualization. For instance, even though killing and rape were considered wrong by almost all subjects, fewer labeled these issues as moral (66% for killing and 62% for rape). In contrast, although a minority of subjects considered homosexuality and abortion wrong, larger numbers labeled them as moral (60% for homosexuality and 61% for abortion). This apparent inconsistency between the evaluation and the labeling of an act may stem from the varying definitions of the term "moral." Spontaneous definitions provided to us by 130 of the 185 subjects yielded four types: 38% defined morality as personal standards or values; 28% defined moral issues as those that are controversial, debated, and publicized (which may explain why some subjects labeled the nonprototypical issues, but not rape and killing, as moral); 14% defined the moral as the socially or religiously acceptable; and 18% defined morality as entailing harm and welfare. Two points need to be stressed here. First, since there was no systematic attempt to elicit subjects' definitions, these data are only suggestive. Second, subjects' evaluations of acts as right or wrong appear to be at least sometimes discrepant with their labeling them as moral issues.

DESIGN AND EXPECTATIONS

As noted previously, this study had three major goals. The first was to examine individuals' reasoning regarding nonprototypical issues. All four issues under study—abortion, homosexuality, pornography, and incest—involve cultural or religious prohibitions on actions that in some way involve sex. Each, however, is also characterized by a number of other features. For instance, abortion involves issues of the definition of life and individual

TABLE 1
Number of Subjects by Issue, Gender, and Age

| | Group 1 | | | | Group 2 | | | | |
| | High School | | College | | High School | | College | | |
Issues	Male	Female	Male	Female	Male	Female	Male	Female	Totals
Nonprototypical:									
Homosexuality	5	4	5	5	7	6	7	8	47
Abortion	11	7	8	4	1	6	7	3	47
Incest	3	0	3	5	6	9	7	5	38
Pornography	7	5	9	6	5	5	8	8	53
									185
Moral:									
Rape	6	4	10	10	12	15	14	9	80
Killing	20	12	15	10	7	11	15	15	105
									185
Personal:									
Nudity at a public beach	3	0	3	3	4	11	11	6	41
Men wearing makeup	12	11	9	8	9	12	11	13	85
Smoking marijuana	11	5	13	9	6	3	7	5	59
									185

TABLE 2

PRESELECTION MEASURE EVALUATIONS (in Percentages) FOR HIGH SCHOOL (N = 87)
AND COLLEGE (N = 98) AGE SUBJECTS

ISSUE	HIGH SCHOOL			COLLEGE		
	Positive	Negative	"Depends"	Positive	Negative	"Depends"
Homosexuality	27	44	29	54	27	20
Abortion	32	12	57	37	17	46
Incest	0	92	8	1	92	7
Pornography	15	52	33	21	42	38
Premarital sex	54	17	29	60	17	23
Killing	0	93	7	0	95	5
Rape	0	99	1	0	100	0
Theft	2	88	9	0	72	28
Nudity at a public beach	26	21	53	35	21	44
Men wearing makeup	34	26	41	56	15	29
Smoking marijuana	34	21	45	47	16	37
Eating horse meat	33	33	35	67	5	28

choice, homosexuality issues of privacy and biological or psychological normality, and pornography issues of privacy, free speech, and how to define social value. Perhaps the most strict cultural taboos apply to incest, even though it is unclear how incest between consenting adults results in harm to persons or society. Our expectation was that, although cultural and religious prohibitions would influence subjects' evaluations and judgments, the particular features and consequences of each of the acts would also be considered.

The second goal was to compare the reasoning of those evaluating non-prototypical issues negatively with the reasoning of those evaluating them positively. This was fulfilled through contrasts in judgments and justifications of Group 1 and Group 2 subjects.

The third goal was to examine the proposition that individuals make different types of judgments (i.e., prescriptive, noncontingent, and generalized vs. nonprescriptive, contingent, and nongeneralized). Assessments of moral and personal issues were included in order to address this proposition. Killing and rape were used because these particular issues clearly fit the definitional criteria for the moral domain and would, therefore, serve to tap noncontingent, generalized prescriptive judgments—if such were part of the subject's reasoning. Since an aspect of the third goal was to determine whether judgments based on personal jurisdiction coexist with either negative or positive evaluations of the nonprototypical issues, we included personal issues that are age appropriate, involve strong explicit or implicit societal prohibitions, and are likely to be viewed as nontrivial. The issues we selected are conventional and/or legally regulated but are also judged by some in this society to be matters of personal discretion. Research has shown that nudity at a public beach is considered to be a socially prohibited act that some regard as being a matter of personal choice and therefore illegitimately regulated (Turiel, 1983). Similarly, the recreational use of drugs like marijuana, although illegal in this country, is often judged as not harmful to others and a matter of personal discretion (Berkowitz et al., in press; Killen, Leviton, & Cahill, 1989; Nucci, Guerra, & Lee, 1989), and cross-gender activities such as men wearing makeup are negatively sanctioned but often judged as matters of personal choice (Stoddart & Turiel, 1985).

This third goal encompasses three interrelated subgoals. One was to compare the reasoning advanced by individuals in judging nonprototypical issues as "morally wrong" with their reasoning about the moral issues. Our expectation was that, in spite of making similar evaluations, subjects would conceptualize the two types of issues differently by showing different criterion judgments and justifications for their negative evaluations. A second subgoal was to ascertain whether subjects who evaluated moral and nonprototypical acts negatively would nevertheless judge certain conventionally prohibited acts to be acceptable and whether their reasoning about those acts would indeed differ from that concerning the moral and nonprototypical issues. The third subgoal was to compare the judgments of subjects who evaluated the nonprototypical issues as acceptable with their judgments about personal issues they saw as acceptable, the aim being to ascertain whether similar judgments would be applied in the two instances. Although here we had no specific expectations, we did expect that these subjects' judgments about moral issues would differ from their judgments about both the personal and the nonprototypical issues.

PROCEDURE AND ASSESSMENTS

In one or two sessions a few days apart, subjects were individually administered a standard set of questions and probes to assess criterion judgments and justifications concerning one nonprototypical, one moral, and one personal issue. The assessments were administered by graduate student assistants. The order nonprototypical-moral-personal was followed so that subjects' judgments about nonprototypical issues—the primary focus of the study—would not be influenced by their responses to the moral and personal issues. These assessments were given immediately following the preselection measure.

The questions used to obtain criterion judgments and justifications are listed in Table 3. First, subjects were asked to evaluate the act (Is the act all right or not all right?). In posing evaluation questions, it was sometimes necessary to specify the circumstances of the acts in order to be sure that subjects were responding to uniform characterizations. The nonprototypical acts in particular required specification of certain circumstances. Thus, homosexuality and incest were presented as situations involving consenting adults, and pornography was presented as excluding child pornography. Abortion was presented as occurring during the first or second trimester; when necessary, it was specified that the pregnancy was not life threatening or due to any kind of coercion.[3]

---

[3] Such controls were important because shifts in circumstances can create essentially different events. For example, a pregnancy that threatens the physical welfare of the mother can be construed as a conflict between two lives and hence give abortion a different meaning than if the mother's life were not in danger. Similarly, the meaning of incest in situations of abuse and coercion of a child by an adult is likely to be construed differently from incest between consenting adults. In their first response to the act evaluation question, 17% of the subjects (all from Group 1) defined the events differently from our controlled versions. These subjects initially gave "depends" responses, taking into account what they judged to be exceptional circumstances of the type just noted; they gave negative evaluations to the acts under the specified circumstances.

TABLE 3

QUESTIONS TO ASSESS CRITERION JUDGMENTS AND JUSTIFICATIONS

1. *Act evaluation.*—Is [issue] all right or not all right? Why or why not?
2. *Legal status in the United States.*—Do you think that there should be a law that prohibits [issue] in this country? Why or why not?
   2a. *Legal contingency.*—Suppose that the majority of people in the United States decided that there [should/should not] be a law that prohibits [issue] and the [law/no law] was in effect. Do you think it would be all right or not all right to [engage in act] if there [were/were not] a law? Why or why not?
3. *Contingency on common practice in the United States.*—Suppose that it [were/were not] common practice for people to [engage in act] in the United States. In that case, do you think it would be all right or not all right to [engage in act]? Why or why not?
4. *Legal status in another country.*—Do you think that there should be a law that prohibits [issue] in all countries? Why or why not?
   4a. *Other country legal contingency.*—Suppose that the majority of people in another country decided that there [should/should not] be a law that prohibits [issue] and [the law/no law] was in effect. Do you think that in that country it would be all right or not all right to [engage in act] if there [were/were not] a law? Why or why not?
5. *Contingency on common practice in another country.*—Suppose that there were another country where it [is/is not] common practice for people to [engage in act]. Do you think that in that country it would be all right or not all right to [engage in act]? Why or why not?

After evaluating the act, subjects were posed a series of questions framed in terms of the cultural context of the United States. They were asked if the act should be legal or illegal (legal status) and then asked to evaluate the act when its legal status was opposite to how they thought it should be (rule or law contingency). Subjects stating that the act should be illegal were asked to evaluate the act if it were legal, and vice versa; this allowed for an assessment of whether the judgment would shift (i.e., was contingent) in accordance with an existing legal situation. To assess whether judgments were contingent on common practice, the questions varied in accordance with the subject's evaluation of the act. Those who had said that the act was "not all right" were asked to evaluate it in the context of places within the United States where (hypothetically) it is generally accepted and practiced; those who said that it was "all right" were asked to evaluate it in cases where it is generally not accepted or practiced. A corresponding set of questions was posed regarding generalizability to other national or cultural contexts. Subjects were first asked if the act should be legal or illegal in all countries; subsequent questions regarding contextual contingency on legal status and common practice also varied according to their response to the question regarding legal status in other countries. Each of the criterion judgment questions included probes (e.g., Why or why not?) to assess justifications (see Table 3).

TABLE 4

SUMMARY DESCRIPTIONS OF JUSTIFICATION CATEGORIES

Category	Description
Simple approval/disapproval . . .	Statement that act is good/right or bad/wrong without elaborated explanation
Custom or tradition	Appeal to family customs or societal customs and traditions
Personal choice	Actor's preferences or prerogatives are legitimate reasons for action
Authority	Appeal to authority expectations, commands, or existence of rules
Prudence	Reference to physical consequences to the actor, which are not imposed by others
Social approval/disapproval	Reference to negative reactions of others toward actor, including social condemnation
Welfare.	Reference to harmful consequences to others
Social coordination	Appeal to the need for social organization or for maintaining a system of shared expectations
Justice and rights	Reference to maintaining a balance of rights between persons
Socialization	Appeal to effects on individuals' later actions, based on naive theories of learning
Deterministic beliefs	Reference to standards dictated by psychological normality, biological order, or religious order
Group contingencies	Deferral of judgment to the act's function in a group or to a consensus within a society

CODING

Three components of the responses were coded: *judgments, justifications,* and *orientation types.* The first two of these were coded with standard and reliable systems used in many previous studies (Turiel et al., 1987). "Judgments" refer to subjects' responses to the criterion judgment questions. Responses to each criterion judgment question were coded as positive (the act is all right or acceptable; should be legal), negative (the act is wrong; should be illegal), and "depends."

Subjects' reasons for each criterion judgment were coded according to a modified scoring system of justification categories first used in Davidson et al. (1983). Brief descriptions of the justification categories are presented in Table 4 (the full coding system, which includes more extensive descriptions and subtypes, is available from the authors). It has been consistently found in previous studies that use of particular categories of justification corresponds with domain: the moral domain is associated with justifications pertaining to welfare, justice, and rights; the conventional domain with justifications pertaining to custom and tradition, authority, social approval, social coordination, and socialization; and the personal realm with personal choice and prudential or pragmatic concerns. Finally, the category "deterministic beliefs" (judgments based on conceptions of psychological, biological, or religious order) was derived from responses made by subjects in this study.

An additional coding system was formulated to categorize the *general orientation types* in regard to the nonprototypical issues. Coding of subjects' judgments and justifications indicated that responses to the nonprototypical issues differed from responses to the prototypical issues (this is detailed in the presentation of the results) as well as from the findings established in previous research on the prototypical issues (on which the coding system for justifications was based). In particular, responses to the nonprototypical issues showed a fair amount of inconsistency and juxtaposition of considerations that are typically not jointly held in the case of prototypical issues. The orientation types were developed in order to capture these inconsistencies and juxtapositions through an analysis of a subject's overall approach to a given nonprototypical issue. The coding scheme was derived from 50% of the protocols and then applied to the remainder. Summary descriptions of the types are given in Appendix A and illustrative excerpts from subjects' responses in Appendix B.

INTERRATER RELIABILITY

To assess coding reliability, a second judge coded, for a randomly chosen 20% of subjects, criterion judgments and justifications for the moral, personal, and nonprototypical issues as well as orientation types for the nonprototypical issues. Cohen's kappa (Cohen, 1960) was .85 for criterion judgments, .76 for justifications, and .82 for orientation types.

RESULTS

To recapitulate, Study 1 was aimed at (*a*) elucidating subjects' concepts of the nonprototypical issues, (*b*) contrasting the concepts underlying negative (Group 1) and positive (Group 2) evaluations of a nonprototypical issue, and (*c*) comparing these concepts with concepts of moral and personal issues. As previously mentioned, the final assignment of subjects (i.e., after preliminary assignments based on the preselection measure) to Groups 1 and 2 was determined by their evaluation of the act in response to the first question of the assessment (see Table 3).[4] All analyses and comparisons focused on codings of criterion judgments, justification categories, and the general orientation types.

ANALYSES OF CRITERION JUDGMENTS

The analyses of responses to criterion judgments are divided into three components. One includes responses to three questions: act evaluation, legal status in the United States, and legal status in another country. With regard to these questions, we examine (a) the effects of specific issues in each issue type and the subject variables sex, age, and group and then (b) findings in relation to the aims and expectations of the study. A second component includes responses reflecting whether judgments were noncontingent and generalized (i.e., evaluation of act if legal/illegal and if common/uncommon practice). The third component entails analyses of patterns of responses by individual subjects based on a subset of criterion judgment questions.

Tables 5 (Group 1) and 6 (Group 2) give an overview of the findings, including the percentage of responses (positive, negative, "depends") for each question, with issues combined by type (moral, personal, and nonprototypical). Except where noted in the text, the frequencies combined by issue type reflect patterns of the individual component issues. These tables show that all subjects in both groups gave negative evaluations of acts in the moral domain and judged that these should be illegal in the United States; almost all (96% in each group) also thought that they should be illegal elsewhere. Furthermore, a large majority maintained their negative evaluation even if such acts were legal or commonplace in either this or other countries. It should be noted that subject selection is not responsible for these findings since *all* preselection responses showed negative evaluations of the acts in the moral domain. By contrast, preselection was responsible for the positive evaluations of personal issues by most subjects in both groups since the issues chosen from the preselection list for further study

[4] There were some changes from the preselection measure to the subsequent act evaluation for the nonprototypical and personal issues but not for the moral issues. With regard to the nonprototypical issues, these were changes from "depends" to "all right" (60% of those who had originally responded with "depends"), from "depends" to "not all right" (40%), and from "not all right" to "all right" (20%). Many of these changes were probably due to the specification of the acts' circumstances when the act evaluation questions were posed. The most frequent change (71%) in responses to the personal issues was from "depends" to "all right" (the large majority of the original "all right" and "not all right" responses remained the same). It is likely that these changes reflect both greater clarity in the presentation of the issues and more reliable assessments of responses in the act evaluations than in the unelaborated responses to the preselection measure.

TABLE 5

Group 1 Responses (in Percentages) to Criterion Judgment Questions

Questions	Moral				Personal				Nonprototypical			
	Positive	Negative	"Depends"	(N)	Positive	Negative	"Depends"	(N)	Positive	Negative	"Depends"	(N)
Act evaluation	0	100	0	(98)	81	3	16	(98)	0	100	0	(98)
Legal status in												
United States	0	100	0	(98)	94	4	2	(98)	56	35	9	(97)
If legal	0	99	1	(96)	33	67	0	(3)	22	61	17	(64)
If illegal	⋯	⋯	⋯	⋯	55	39	7	(93)	66	14	21	(29)
If common	1	97	2	(96)	33	68	0	(3)	14	66	20	(64)
If uncommon	⋯	⋯	⋯	⋯	92	5	3	(94)	91	6	3	(32)
Legal status in												
another country	2	96	2	(97)	96	3	1	(94)	70	23	8	(93)
If legal	1	95	4	(98)	0	100	0	(2)	32	51	17	(59)
If illegal	⋯	⋯	⋯	⋯	58	41	1	(90)	67	24	9	(33)
If common	2	94	4	(98)	0	100	0	(2)	29	54	18	(63)
If uncommon	⋯	⋯	⋯	⋯	93	4	2	(90)	87	3	10	(30)

Issue Type

TABLE 6

GROUP 2 RESPONSES (in Percentages) to CRITERION JUDGMENT QUESTIONS

| | ISSUE TYPE | | | | | | | | | | | |
| | Moral | | | | Personal | | | | Nonprototypical | | | |
QUESTIONS	Positive	Negative	"Depends"	(N)	Positive	Negative	"Depends"	(N)	Positive	Negative	"Depends"	(N)
Act evaluation	0	100	0	(87)	86	2	12	(87)	100	0	0	(87)
Legal status in United States	0	100	0	(87)	99	1	0	(87)	100	0	0	(87)
If legal	0	100	0	(85)	100	0	0	(1)	...	...	...	...
If illegal	...	...	...	...	74	21	5	(84)	84	10	6	(83)
If common	0	98	2	(86)	100	0	0	(1)	...	...	...	...
If uncommon	...	...	...	...	97	2	1	(85)	100	0	0	(83)
Legal status in another country	2	96	1	(85)	98	1	1	(87)	100	0	0	(85)
If legal	4	94	2	(83)	100	0	0	(1)	...	...	...	...
If illegal	...	...	...	...	74	24	2	(85)	88	11	1	(84)
If common	4	88	8	(86)	100	0	0	(1)	...	...	...	...
If uncommon	...	...	...	...	96	2	1	(84)	99	0	1	(83)

were ones that subjects had evaluated positively. (No subject gave negative evaluations to all personal issues listed on the preselection measure; hence, none were excluded for this reason. The few subjects who gave negative or "depends" responses on the act evaluation were those who changed their evaluations from the preselection measure.) There was group variation in judgments of nonprototypical issues; here, however, some differences between Groups 1 and 2 reflect elements of the subject selection procedure. Recall that group assignment was based on subjects' evaluations (negative or positive) of a nonprototypical act listed on the preselection measure.

Effects of sex, age, group, and issue.—The first analyses were aimed at determining whether subject variables have an effect on responses to the questions concerning the evaluation and legal status of the act. It was expected that there would be no sex or age effects on these criterion judgments but that there would be a main effect for group. We also examined the effects of specific issues, with the expectation that differences might occur only among the nonprototypical issues.

Responses to these questions were analyzed by means of a log-linear approach, using a logit analysis in which models are generated that predict the response on a specified dependent variable (i.e., the act evaluation and the legal status questions) as a function of various combinations of the specified independent variables (Goodman, 1972; Magidson, 1978). The first step in this procedure was to test the degree to which a model including only the main effects of age, issue, and group fit the data (such a model was chosen as a starting point because analyses of the saturated models—which included all main and interaction effects—indicated that there were no significant interaction effects for any of the questions). Following a stepwise hierarchical procedure, other models were then systematically tested to determine the contribution of each parameter (i.e., age, issue, or group) to the fit. This procedure involves subtracting the chi-square value obtained in testing the general model from the chi-square value obtained under the reduced model, in which the effect of one of the parameters is omitted. The resultant chi-square value estimates the magnitude of the main effect for the omitted variable (because there was so little variance in subjects' responses to the moral issues, only the personal and nonprototypical issues were submitted to this analysis). In initial analyses, sex was included as one of the parameters. However, since it had no effect in any of the analyses, this parameter was deleted in order to increase cell frequencies.

For each of the six questions (three questions per personal and nonprototypical issue type), chi-square values of the general model and the separate main effect contributions resulting from the log-linear analyses are presented in Table 7. (Analysis of the nonprototypical act evaluation did not include group or issue as parameters since subject group assignment was based on these responses; in this case, the general model included only the

TABLE 7

SUMMARY OF LOG-LINEAR ANALYSES FOR THE MAIN EFFECTS OF AGE, ISSUE, AND GROUP ON CRITERION JUDGMENTS

CRITERION JUDGMENTS	TEST OF THE GENERAL MODEL			MAIN EFFECTS OF AGE			MAIN EFFECTS OF ISSUE			MAIN EFFECTS OF GROUP		
	χ^2	df	p	χ^2_R	df	p	χ^2_R	df	p	χ^2_R	df	p
Personal:												
Act evaluation	3.58	7	N.S.	.50	1	N.S.	2.68	2	N.S.	1.23	1	N.S.
Legal status in United States	.97	4	N.S.	0	1	N.S.	11.38	5	< .05	4.78	1	< .05
Legal status in another country	1.30	4	N.S.	.24	1	N.S.	9.18	5	N.S.	2.20	1	N.S.
Nonprototypical:												
Act evaluation	4.20	3	N.S.	.05	1	N.S.	...	...	...	...	...	...
Legal status in United States	4.79	3	N.S.	.38	1	N.S.	17.18	3	< .05	52.93	8	< .05
Legal status in another country	8.43	3	< .05	2.22	1	N.S.	1.50	3	N.S.	34.22	8	< .05

NOTE.—χ^2_R refers to chi-square values resulting from the logit analysis examining separate parameter contributions to the variance. For log-linear analyses, response categories were collapsed into (1) positive and (2) negative plus "depends." The differences in degrees of freedom were due to structural zero marginals.

main effects of age.) The results indicate that, for the nonprototypical issues, the general model, which includes overall main effects for age, issue, and group, provides a parsimonious fit of the data on all but the legal status in another country question. For this question, a model including only the group main effect provided the most parsimonious fit of the data.

For the personal issues, the parameters of age, issue, and group had no significant effects on subjects' evaluation of the acts or on their judgments about legal status in another country. (The findings on the act evaluations for each parameter follow from the preselection procedures since only positively evaluated personal issues were chosen.) Judgments of legal status in the United States were not associated with age, but there were significant effects of both particular personal issue and groups. Although there was a significant main effect for issue on legal status in the United States, the large majority of subjects nevertheless said that each of the personal issues should be legal in the United States. Whereas 100% said so about men wearing makeup, 92% and 95% of subjects made that judgment regarding marijuana and nudity, respectively. A contrast based on the log-linear model (Marascuilo & Busk, 1987) showed the difference between the latter two to be nonsignificant. The main effect appears to arise from the difference between responses to the makeup and the marijuana issues; however, absence of variation in the makeup issue precludes statistical comparison. Similarly, although the main effect for group was significant, the large majority of subjects in both groups—99% of Group 2 and 94% of Group 1—judged that the personal issues should be legal in the United States.

The log-linear analysis of the nonprototypical acts showed no significant age differences on any of the three questions (the finding for the act evaluation question follows from the preselection). Significant main effects for issue were found in the legal status in the United States question. This difference was due solely to Group 1 responses since there was no variation in responses of Group 2 subjects. Among Group 1 subjects, 67% judged that incest, 36% that pornography, 24% that abortion, and 11% that homosexuality should be illegal. Post hoc pairwise contrasts indicated that judgments about incest and homosexuality were significantly different ($z = 3.88$, $p < .05$). Significant between-group differences were obtained in judgments about the legal status of nonprototypical acts in the United States and elsewhere. All Group 2 subjects judged that these acts should be legal in the United States and elsewhere; in Group 1, 56% judged that they should be legal in the United States and 70% that they should be legal in another country.

Since the log-linear analyses showed no effects of subjects' sex or age, these variables were not included in subsequent analyses of criterion judgments. The log-linear analyses also showed that, for the most part, judgments about particular items within issue types did not differ; an exception was in judgments regarding legal status in the United States of incest and homosexuality. Finally, judgments concerning the moral and personal domains were similar for Groups 1 and 2, but the groups did differ in judgments concerning the nonprototypical issues even on dimensions (the two legal status questions) other than that by which group assignments were made.

Comparisons among issue types.—In the following analyses of the three criterion judgment questions, we examined differences among subjects' judgments concerning the moral, personal, and nonprototypical issues. Based on our hypothesis of coexisting judgments, we expected responses to the three issue types to differ.

Comparisons of the act evaluation and legal status questions among issue types were conducted using the Stuart test (Zwick, Neuhoff, Marascuilo, & Levin, 1982), which entails a set of planned pairwise comparisons (according to the Dunn-Bonferroni approach) of the distribution of marginal probabilities.[5] The critical values for each contrast, with the alpha level at .05, are $z = \pm 2.40$ for two-tailed tests and $z = \pm 2.13$ for one-tailed tests (these critical values were also used for all subsequent Stuart test analyses). The alpha levels were distributed across the three contrasts (positive, negative, "depends") within each comparison. Comparisons between the personal and the nonprototypical issues were two tailed, whereas comparisons of the moral issues with the personal or nonprototypical ones were one tailed.[6]

[5] Typically, the Stuart test is used in conjunction with the Bowker test. These tests measure change across correlated proportions for qualitative, multilevel variables, with one testing for marginal homogeneity (Stuart) and the other for internal symmetry (Bowker). However, we report only the results of the Stuart tests since for our purposes the Bowker statistic does not provide additional information regarding changes in response across the variables examined. That is, we were more interested in the pattern of overall responses (negative, positive, "depends") to a question across domains (marginal homogeneity) than in changes within particular responses across domains (internal symmetry).

[6] Given the finding (reported in the previous section) of a significant difference between two of the nonprototypical issues, additional analyses compared each nonprototypical act with issues combined for the moral domain to test the expectation that reasoning about the moral domain would differ from reasoning about each of the nonprototypical issues. Using the Stuart test, we found that responses to each of the three nonprototypical issues differed significantly from responses to the moral domain in the expected direction. Subjects were more likely to evaluate the moral issues negatively and to judge that they should be illegal (in both the United States and another country). The nonprototypical issues were not expected to differ necessarily on all dimensions from those in the personal domain since subjects judging the former positively were included in the study (Group 2). For the most part, subjects evaluated personal issues more positively than nonprototypical issues and were more likely to judge that they should be legal.

A perusal of Table 5 suggests that the judgments of Group 1 subjects differed by issue type. In the moral domain, all the subjects evaluated the acts negatively and judged that they should be illegal in the United States; a large majority (96%) also said that they should be illegal in another country. In contrast, acts in the personal domain were evaluated positively by all and judged that they should be legal both in the United States and elsewhere by most. Stuart tests performed to compare the proportions of differing responses showed that, for act evaluations, positive and "depends" responses were more likely for the personal than for the moral acts ($z = 20.18$ and 4.39, respectively) and that negative responses were more likely for moral than for personal ones ($z = 55.71$). Correspondingly, personal acts were more often judged as appropriately legal (in the United States, $z = 38.76$; in another country, $z = 36.72$) and moral acts as illegal (in the United States, $z = 47.99$; in another country, $z = 33.80$).

Table 5 also shows that the configuration of Group 1 responses for the nonprototypical acts differs from the configurations of responses to the moral and personal acts. For nonprototypical acts only, despite their negative evaluations, the majority of Group 1 subjects nevertheless judged that the acts should be legal both in the United States and in another country. Summarizing significant results obtained by means of Stuart tests, we found that moral acts were more often judged to be appropriately illegal than nonprototypical acts. It was also found that personal acts were evaluated positively and judged as appropriately legal to a greater extent than nonprototypical ones.[7]

The data for Group 2 show a difference between responses to the moral issues, on the one hand, and the personal and nonprototypical issues, on the other (see Table 6). Although significantly more subjects gave positive evaluations of the nonprototypical than the personal acts ($z = 3.73$), the large majority (86%) also evaluated the latter positively (all evaluated the nonprototypical acts positively). There were no significant differences between the two issue types in judgments that these acts should be legal both in the United States and in another country. In contrast, all comparisons

---

[7] Results from several Stuart tests pertain to this summarization. The following comparisons between the moral and the nonprototypical issue types were significant: more subjects judged that the nonprototypical acts should be legal in the United States ($z = 11.04$) and in another country ($z = 13.15$) and that the moral acts should be illegal in the United States ($z = 13.41$) and in another country ($z = 15.70$). The following comparisons between the personal and the nonprototypical issue types were significant: more positive and "depends" evaluations were given of personal acts ($z = 20.18$ and 4.37, respectively) and more negative evaluations of the nonprototypical ones ($z = 55.71$); more subjects judged that the personal acts should be legal in the United States ($z = 7.42$) and in another country ($z = 5.43$) and that the nonprototypical acts should be illegal in the United States ($z = 6.06$) and in another country ($z = 4.75$).

between the moral and the personal as well as between the moral and the nonprototypical proved to be significant.[8]

Finally, the interaction between issue type and group was tested by means of an extension of the Stuart test (Zwick et al., 1982). This analysis permits comparison of the two groups on the magnitude of obtained differences between issue types and determination of their significance. Thus, each test of interaction examines whether, within a particular comparison (e.g., moral vs. nonprototypical), the difference in proportion of responses obtained in Group 1 is statistically different from the differences seen in Group 2. For the two questions on legality, significant differences within each group had been obtained between the moral and the nonprototypical acts as well as between the personal and the nonprototypical ones. The current analysis shows that the direction and magnitude of these within-group differences (see Tables 5 and 6) were significantly different in Groups 1 and 2 (z's ranging from 5.61 to 41.98). In comparisons between the moral and the personal issues, the group-by-category interactions were not significant.

Contingency and generalization responses.—The analyses of responses to the act evaluation and the two legal status questions showed that criterion judgments differ by issue type: Group 1 judgments about each issue type differed from the others, whereas Group 2 judgments about moral issues differed from those about nonprototypical and personal issues. In this section, we examine responses to these and additional questions reflecting judgments of "contingency" and "generalizability" (see the questions in Table 3).

The data presented in Tables 5 and 6 indicate that, for acts in the moral domain, subjects in both groups made judgments that are noncontingent and generalizable. The negative evaluations of such acts included the conception that they should be legally restricted in one's own country and in other countries. Furthermore, nearly all subjects stated that these acts would be wrong even if legal or commonly practiced (for Groups 1 and 2, respec-

---

[8] The following comparisons between the moral and the personal domains were significant: more positive and "depends" evaluations were given of the personal acts ($z = 23.32$ and 3.36, respectively), and more negative evaluations were given of the moral ones ($z = 60.80$); more subjects judged that the personal acts should be legal than judged that the moral acts should be legal in the United States ($z = 86.50$) and in another country ($z = 48.20$) and that the moral acts should be illegal in the United States ($z = 86.50$) and in another country ($z = 41.49$). With regard to comparisons between the moral and the nonprototypical issue types, no statistical tests were computed for responses to the act evaluation and legal status in the United States questions because all subjects evaluated the moral acts negatively and judged that they should be illegal in the United States and all evaluated the nonprototypical acts positively and judged they should be legal in the United States. Questioned about another country, more subjects judged that nonprototypical acts should be legal ($z = 58.69$) and that the moral acts should be illegal ($z = 47.62$).

tively, 99% and 100% stated that these acts would be wrong if legal in the United States, 97% and 98% wrong if commonly practiced in the United States, 95% and 94% wrong if legal in other countries, and 94% and 88% wrong if commonly practiced in other countries).

Judgments about the personal domain were more varied (see Tables 5 and 6). First, whereas a large majority of subjects maintained their positive evaluations of the acts even if their practice were uncommon in the United States (92% for Group 1 and 97% for Group 2), fewer (though still a majority) did so in the context of assuming their illegal status in the United States (55% and 74%, respectively). Stuart tests showed that these differences between responses to the illegal and the uncommon practice contingency questions were significant within each group (Group 1: $z = 7.64$ for positive and 6.10 for negative responses; Group 2: $z = 4.66$ for positive and 4.14 for negative responses). The same pattern prevailed when subjects were questioned about another country: a greater proportion maintained their positive evaluations of the personal acts in the context of uncommon practice (93% for Group 1 and 96% for Group 2) than in the context of illegality (58% for Group 1 and 74% for Group 2). These differences were significant (Group 1: $z = 5.61$ for positive and 5.77 for negative responses; Group 2: $z = 4.62$ for both positive and negative responses). Second, responses to the legal contingency questions also showed some between-group differences (see Tables 5 and 6). In Group 1, a majority of the subjects evaluated the personal acts positively even if they were illegal in the United States (55%) or elsewhere (58%); the comparable proportions for Group 2 were 74% for each question. The significance of the between-group difference on legal contingency is $\chi^2(2) = 7.03$, $p < .05$, in the United States and $\chi^2(2) = 6.32$, $p < .05$, in another country.

With regard to the nonprototypical acts, the contingency and generalization responses were straightforward in Group 2 but not in Group 1. Having evaluated the acts positively, Group 2 subjects stated that these acts should be legal and maintained their positive evaluations even if the acts were either illegal or uncommon in the United States or in another country (Table 6). Group 1 responses differed in that a substantial number of subjects judged that the acts they had evaluated negatively should nevertheless be legal. This complicated the analyses because the contingency questions (i.e., what if it were illegal/not common practice) have a different meaning to subjects who juxtapose a negative evaluation with the judgment that the act should be legal than to those evaluating the act positively and judging that it should be legal. For those who evaluated the act positively and judge that it should be legal, the contingency questions pose an alternative to their legality judgment (i.e., what if it were illegal) to ascertain if this changes their evaluation of the act. Subjects who evaluate the act negatively and judge that it should be legal gave two responses indicating that they do not

TABLE 8

PERCENTAGES OF GROUP 1 SUBJECTS (N = 98) GIVING
CONTINGENT AND NONGENERALIZED RESPONSES TO QUESTIONS
REGARDING NONPROTOTYPICAL ACTS

Questions	%
In the United States:	
Act should be legal	55
If legal, act is all right	6
If common practice, act is all right	3
Total	64
In another country:	
Act should be legal	13
If legal, act is all right	3
If common practice, act is all right	0
Total	16
Total for United States and another country	81

NOTE.—The results for "in another country" include only subjects who did not give contingent and nongeneralized responses to questions framed "in the United States"; in total, 76% gave contingent and nongeneralized responses to questions concerning another country.

regard the issue as noncontingent (which would entail the judgments that the act should be illegal and is wrong even if legal). It appears that, even though the act is regarded as wrong, the subject views its performance as "contingent" on the actor's choice (the justification data presented below support this interpretation).

To be sure, this is a different form of contingency from the typical evaluation of an act as contingent on its legal status. Because the judgments in question are clearly different from noncontingent judgments and entail a type of contingency (i.e., on individual choice), we included them in tallies of contingent and/or nongeneralized responses. Accordingly, we tallied the number of subjects who (1) judged that the negatively evaluated act should be legal and/or (2) judged that the act should be illegal but would evaluate it positively if it were to be legal or common practice. The results, which are presented in Table 8, show that a large majority of Group 1 subjects judged the nonprototypical acts as contingent and/or nongeneralizable to other contexts in at least one of the two conditions. In Group 1, therefore, there is a clear difference between subjects' criterion judgments about nonprototypical and moral acts.

Criterion judgment patterns.—Additional analyses were undertaken to ascertain whether the group findings are applicable to individual subjects' patterns of criterion judgment responses. The following four distinct response patterns emerged from responses concerning act evaluation, legal status, and legal status contingency (i.e., evaluation of the act if it were legal/

TABLE 9

RESPONSE PATTERNS (in Percentages) FOR EACH GROUP BY DOMAINS
AND NONPROTOTYPICAL ISSUES

PATTERNS	MORAL		PERSONAL		NONPROTOTYPICAL	
	Group 1	Group 2	Group 1	Group 2	Group 1	Group 2
A (noncontingently negative)	100	100	2	0	28	0
B (contingently positive or negative)	0	0	42	21	7	16
C (noncontingently positive)	0	0	54	77	0	84
D (wrong and legal)	0	0	1	3	65	0

illegal).[9] In *Pattern A,* the subject evaluated the act negatively, judged that it should be illegal, and evaluated it negatively even if it were legal (responses were negative in a noncontingent way). As Table 9 shows, this pattern characterized all subjects' responses for the moral domain. It was also used by 28% of Group 1 subjects for nonprototypical acts. *Pattern B* included subjects evaluating the act as positive, negative, or "depends" in conjunction with a legality judgment of contingency (responses were positive or negative in contingent ways). Thus, positive act evaluations were coupled with a negative evaluation if the act were illegal, negative evaluations with the judgment that it should be illegal as well as with a positive evaluation if it were legal, and evaluations of "depends" with the judgment that the act should be legal as well as with its negative evaluation if it were illegal. This pattern pertained to the personal and nonprototypical issue types. In *Pattern C,* the subject evaluated the act either positively or "depends," judged that it should be legal, and evaluated it positively even if it were illegal (responses were positive in a noncontingent way). This too characterized the personal and nonprototypical issue types. Finally, in *Pattern D,* the subject evaluated the act negatively and judged that it should be

[9] Patterns based on the four criterion judgment questions captured the responses of the large majority of subjects. Including the other questions in the construction of the patterns would have yielded similar results, with only each of a few additional patterns containing very few subjects. Also, some subjects were excluded either because they did not respond to one of the questions or because their responses did not constitute a coherent pattern. Missing responses occurred in four moral, four personal, and six nonprototypical issues. Patterns could not be derived because subjects gave "depends" responses on two or three of the questions in four cases for the personal domain and two cases for the nonprototypical issues. Additionally, in four cases (three personal and one nonprototypical), the response patterns across questions were not coherent.

legal. Substantive use of this pattern was shown only by Group 1 subjects for the nonprototypical acts.

This association of subject response patterns with issue types is consistent with the group analyses. Stuart tests (critical value at ± 2.79) revealed that Pattern A was used significantly more by both groups for the moral than for either the personal ($z = 96.69$) or the nonprototypical issues ($z = 33.59$). Pattern A was also used significantly more for the nonprototypical than for the personal issues, which is entirely accounted for by the responses of Group 1 ($z = 4.96$). Patterns B and C were used significantly more by all subjects in the personal than in the moral domain ($z = 8.92$ and 17.62, respectively); within Group 1, these two patterns were also used significantly more in the personal domain than for the nonprototypical issues ($z = 6.18$ and 10.01, respectively). The significantly greater use of Pattern D with the nonprototypical issues than in the moral or personal domains is accounted for by its use in Group 1 ($z = 12.57$ and 12.02, respectively).

The only significant age difference was that, for the nonprototypical acts, high school subjects used Pattern B to a greater extent than college subjects (21% vs. 3%, $z = 3.44$). With regard to particular nonprototypical acts, Pattern C was used more for abortion (66%) than for incest (22%, $z = 4.32$).

ASSESSMENTS OF JUSTIFICATIONS

Subjects' explanations for their criterion judgments were elicited through systematic probes associated with each question and coded according to the categories summarized in Table 4. Each justification category can apply to either positive or negative responses to the criterion judgment questions. Subjects sometimes gave more than one type of justification for each question; in such instances, all justifications were coded and weighted according to their numbers (i.e., two justifications for one criterion judgment were weighted .5 each, three were weighted .33 each, etc.). Multiple justifications that included consideration of reasons for the positive and negative sides of the issue were also coded and represented in the results.

We first present findings on the use of justification categories for the moral (Table 10) and personal (Table 11) domains; ages and issues are combined since there were virtually no differences between the age groups or among issues within either domain. Only responses to the act evaluation and legal status in the United States questions are presented because these were the responses that were most fully elaborated. As questions proceeded, subjects gave less fully elaborated responses (i.e., in the "simple approval/

TABLE 10

JUSTIFICATION RESPONSES (in Percentages) FOR THE MORAL DOMAIN

	GROUPS AND QUESTIONS			
	Group 1		Group 2	
CATEGORIES	Act Evaluation	Legal Status in United States	Act Evaluation	Legal Status in United States
Simple approval/ disapproval	9	15	5	9
Custom and tradition ...	2	0	0	0
Authority	0	20	0	35
Prudence	0	8	0	0
Welfare	7	3	8	3
Social coordination	0	0	0	1
Justice and rights	81	52	87	51
Deterministic beliefs	1	0	0	0
N	98	97	87	86

TABLE 11

JUSTIFICATION RESPONSES (in Percentages) FOR THE PERSONAL DOMAIN

	GROUPS AND QUESTIONS			
	Group 1		Group 2	
CATEGORIES	Act Evaluation	Legal Status in United States	Act Evaluation	Legal Status in United States
Simple approval/ disapproval	14	22	14	30
Custom and tradition ...	1 (8)	0	1 (7)	0
Personal choice	50	57	62	49
Authority	0	1 (2)	0	0 (1)
Prudence	0 (5)	0 (1)	0	0
Welfare	19	14	16	19
Socialization	0	0 (1)	0	0
Deterministic beliefs	0 (1)	0	0	0
Group contingencies	0 (1)	0 (1)	0	0
N	98	98	87	86

NOTE.—Justifications for negative evaluations and illegality responses are in parentheses.

disapproval" category) because they felt that they had already justified their positions in the first two questions.

The data in Table 10 show that Groups 1 and 2 gave similar justifications for the moral domain and that "justice and rights" was the most frequently used category. The table also shows that a minority of subjects (20% in Group 1 and 35% in Group 2) used the "authority" category to justify the judgment that the acts should be illegal (the majority of elaborated responses to the subsequent questions, which are not shown in Table 10, were in the "justice and rights" category). The most frequently used category for the personal domain was "personal choice" (see Table 11), and the majority of elaborated responses to subsequent questions were also in that category. For the personal domain, all responses in the "welfare" category (19% in Group 1 and 16% in Group 2) were instances in which subjects invoked the absence of harm as a justification for the evaluation of the act (e.g., "it is all right because it does not hurt anyone").

It is evident that the justifications for the moral and personal domains differed from each other and in each case clustered around a limited number of expected categories consistent with previous studies. Because of the clear-cut nature of the clustering of justifications for the moral and personal domains, statistical analyses were not conducted on any of the justifications. Unlike the moral and personal domains, justifications among the particular nonprototypical acts appear to differ. Tables 12 and 13 present the justifications for each nonprototypical issue for Groups 1 and 2, respectively. Whereas Group 1 justifications for their evaluations of homosexuality fall mainly in two categories ("custom and tradition" and "deterministic beliefs"), the spread of justifications for evaluations of the other three issues was larger (see Table 12). Note that the use of these justifications differs from the use of "justice and rights" as the main category to justify negative evaluations of acts in the moral domain. As expected, however, moral justifications in the form of the "welfare" category were used by a substantial number of subjects with regard to abortion (the welfare of the unborn child) to explain negative evaluations of the act. Also note that responses to the legal status questions had a substantial number of justifications for the judgment that the acts should be legal.

Group 2 (Table 13) also showed a range of justifications for each of the nonprototypical acts. Justifications of homosexuality showed the greatest distribution across categories; the most frequently used category for abortion was "prudence," whereas "personal choice" was the most frequent for incest and pornography. The "welfare" category was used to some extent in justifying positive evaluations of homosexuality, pornography, and incest. As within the personal domain, this entailed reasoning that the act is all right because of the absence of harm.

TABLE 12

GROUP 1 JUSTIFICATION RESPONSES (in Percentages) for NONPROTOTYPICAL ISSUES

ISSUES AND QUESTIONS

CATEGORIES	Homosexuality		Abortion		Incest		Pornography	
	Act Evaluation	Legal Status in United States	Act Evaluation	Legal Status in United States	Act Evaluation	Legal Status in United States	Act Evaluation	Legal Status in United States
Simple approval/ disapproval	0	7	0	20	0	0	0	0
		(4)	(13)	(7)	(15)	(19)	(17)	(4)
Custom and tradition	0	0	0	0	0	0	0	0
	(32)	(5)	(9)		(27)	(12)	(8)	(12)
Personal choice	4	32	6	7	6	15	8	15
Authority	0	2	0	0	0	4	0	4
		(2)	(6)	(3)	(2)	(27)		(12)
Prudence	0	1	6	30	0	6	4	8
					(10)		(43)	(6)
Welfare	2	12	3	7	2	3	0	15
			(50)	(13)	(4)		(2)	
Social coordination	0	0	0	0	0	0	0	2
					(4)	(6)	(2)	
Justice and rights	2	21	0	10	0	0	0	10
			(6)	(3)				
Socialization	0	0	0	0	0	0	0	0
	(5)	(4)						
Deterministic beliefs	0	0	0	0	0	0	0	0
	(55)	(2)	(6)		(31)	(4)	(16)	(13)
N	28	28	16	15	27	27	24	26

NOTE.—Justifications for negative evaluations and illegality responses are in parentheses.

TABLE 13

GROUP 2 JUSTIFICATION RESPONSES (in Percentages) for NONPROTOTYPICAL ISSUES

	ISSUES AND QUESTIONS							
	Homosexuality		Abortion		Incest		Pornography	
CATEGORIES	Act Evaluation	Legal Status in United States	Act Evaluation	Legal Status in United States	Act Evaluation	Legal Status in United States	Act Evaluation	Legal Status in United States
Simple approval/ disapproval	16	16	0	13	14	45	11	26
Custom and tradition	3 (7)	0	0	0	0 (14)	0	2 (5)	0
Personal choice	18	37	28	53	59	18	43	37
Authority	0	0	0	3	0	0	0	0
Prudence	11 (3)	0	41 (1)	12	0	0	6 (2)	2
Social approval/ disapproval	0	0	0	0	0	0	0	0
Welfare	21	21	21 (2)	8	14	18	23 (2)	20
Justice and rights	10	26	8	10	0	18	4	15
Deterministic beliefs	13	0	0	0	0	0	2 (1)	0
N	19	19	30	30	11	11	27	27

NOTE.—Justifications for negative evaluations and illegality responses are in parentheses.

ORIENTATIONS

Because of the within-subject variation in justification categories for nonprototypical acts, six general orientation types were derived, based on global analyses of subjects' protocols. (For a description of the orientation types, see App. A; for illustrative excerpts from subject protocols, see App. B.) The Moral orientation (Type A) reflects an application of concepts of welfare, fairness, or rights and generally includes noncontingent and generalized act evaluations. As shown in Table 14, this orientation type was seen infrequently by itself and used only by Group 1 subjects for the act of abortion. The Normative Model orientation (Type B) refers to the use of assumptions about normal functioning (natural, supernatural, biological, psychological, or societal) to make prescriptive judgments about the acts. The Normative Model orientation was also seen infrequently by itself and used only by Group 1. The Consequential orientation (Type C) entails judgments that focus on negative effects or consequences of the act on either social organization or psychological functioning; again, it was used infrequently by itself (only by Group 1 subjects in reference to pornography and incest). The Personal orientation (Type D), in which the acts are viewed as within the realm of personal jurisdiction, was the only orientation frequently used by itself (the majority of Group 2 subjects).

The Juxtaposition orientation (Type E) was used by the majority of Group 1 subjects in reasoning about each of the nonprototypical acts. In these cases, a Type A, B, or C orientation—entailing prescriptive judgments about wrongness—was combined with the judgment that the act is under personal jurisdiction or relative to cultural contexts and thus should be left to the discretion of individuals or societies. The Moral and Personal orientations were juxtaposed mainly for the act of abortion, and the Normative Model orientation was juxtaposed with the Personal most frequently in the case of homosexuality. The last orientation (Type F, Unelaborated) reflected prescriptive judgments that were largely unelaborated; it occurred mainly in the case of incest (23%) on the part of Group 1 subjects.

The between-group differences in prevalence of different orientations were significant. To obtain sufficient frequencies in each cell, chi-square analyses were based on comparisons among the Personal orientation, the Juxtaposition orientation, and all other orientations combined. Group 1 showed significantly greater use of the Juxtaposition orientation, whereas Group 2 used the Personal orientation more, $\chi^2(2) = 138.89, p < .0001$.

DISCUSSION

The findings of Study 1 serve to elucidate how individuals conceptualize the nonprototypical issues and support our general proposition of coex-

TABLE 14

General Orientation Types (in Percentages) for Nonprototypical Issues as Divided by Group

	Group and Issue							
	Group 1				Group 2			
Orientations	Homosexuality	Abortion	Incest	Pornography	Homosexuality	Abortion	Incest	Pornography
Type A (Moral)	0	17	0	0	0	0	0	0
Type B (Normative Model)	14	0	8	12	0	0	0	0
Type C (Consequential) ...	0	0	8	8	0	0	0	0
Type D (Personal)	0	6	0	12	84	93	91	92
Type E (Juxtaposition)	86	77	62	65	16	7	9	8
Type F (Unelaborated)	0	0	23	4	0	0	0	0
N	28	17	26	26	19	30	11	26

istence, namely, that individuals maintain different types of judgments about different domains or types of issues. Within-subject variations were obtained in each group. One such variation was that judgments and justifications differed between the nonprototypical and the moral issues. We also obtained group differences in reasoning about the nonprototypical issues along with group similarities in reasoning about the moral issues. The former result, of course, must be interpreted in the context of our preselection of subjects and issues. Confirming the public opinion surveys, there was a division between those who evaluated the nonprototypical issues negatively (Group 1) and those who did not (Group 2). Moreover, along with these different evaluations of the nonprototypical acts, there were group differences in criterion judgments, justifications, and orientation types. Again, we note that the group similarities in judgments about the moral issues cannot be attributed to the preselection procedure since all participants responded in the same ways; thus, these findings can be interpreted in the same way as those of previous studies on moral issues.

First, we consider the configuration of coexisting judgments among Group 2 subjects. These subjects' responses to the nonprototypical issues clearly contrasted with their responses to the moral issues. The large majority evaluated the nonprototypical acts positively and maintained that type of judgment even if the acts were illegal or uncommon in one's own or another country. They also judged that these acts should not be legally restricted. Their justifications were mainly that the acts are under personal jurisdiction, are not harmful to others, and bear only on consequences to the actor (prudence). In terms of orientation types, most were characterized by a Personal orientation (Type D), viewing the nonprototypical acts as primarily matters of individual choice.

Group 2 subjects' conceptualization of the personal issues was similar: personal issues were also evaluated positively across contexts and reasoned about in terms of personal choice. Nevertheless, subjects in this group cannot be characterized as concerned solely with individual choice, freedoms, and negation of legal jurisdiction since, in their responses to the issues in the moral domain, all upheld the necessity for legal restrictions on the basis of the importance of ensuring justice and maintaining rights.

Group 1 subjects also displayed a coexistence of different social judgments, although with configurations among issue types differing from those of Group 2. Specifically, the two groups made similar judgments concerning the moral and personal domains and differed only with respect to the nonprototypical issues. In their judgments about the personal issues, subjects in Group 1 were oriented to individual choice and freedoms. Their conceptualization of these issues was in most respects similar to the ways in which Group 2 subjects conceptualized both the personal and the nonprototypical issues. This is to say not that the two groups would necessarily reason similarly about *all* personal issues but rather that they reasoned similarly about *some* issues and that concerns with personal jurisdiction were part of the social reasoning of each group (note also that the two groups did not differ in their conceptualization of the moral issues).

The findings for Group 1 subjects confirm our expectation that reasoning about moral issues would differ from reasoning about nonprototypical issues even when those acts are evaluated negatively and labeled as "moral." That is, individuals' seemingly "moral" evaluations about nonprototypical issues differ from *their own* moral judgments about other issues. On the one hand, individuals' judgments about the moral issues were consistent in that negative act evaluations were combined with noncontingency and generalizability, all justified on the grounds of justice and rights. On the other hand, judgments about negatively evaluated nonprototypical issues were combined with the judgments that they should not be legally restricted in either this or another country. Moreover, the majority judged the nonprototypical acts to be contingent on legal status or common practice grounds and to lack generalizability to other social contexts.

Evaluating nonprototypical acts as wrong and judging that they should not be legally regulated does differ from responses to the prototypical moral issues. However, this combination of responses does not in itself necessarily mean that subjects were not taking a "moral" stance to the nonprototypical issues. It may be that one can regard an act as morally wrong and at the same time believe that, for one reason or another, it would be best if the state did not interfere (e.g., for reasons of efficiency or that state regulation is even worse than the offence). The question of whether subjects take a moral stance with that particular combination raises further questions of labeling and categorization that cannot be resolved here. Two points need to be stressed, however. First, subjects did not generally consider legal regulation undesirable; they accepted its legitimacy for the moral issues. Second, criteria other than the undesirability of legal regulation were applied to the nonprototypical issues, including that they are not contingent on legal status or common practices in different social contexts.

Moreover, justifications for the nonprototypical issues differed from those for the moral issues. The "justice and rights" and "welfare" categories were not used extensively for the nonprototypical issues; the category used most frequently by Group 1 subjects was "deterministic beliefs"—a category rarely used by them for the other issue types or by Group 2 subjects. This justification entails a comparison of the act to normal psychological, biological, or religious-based functioning; the acts were evaluated negatively on the grounds that they deviated from presumed normality or order in these systems.

Further details about these Group 1 subjects' reasoning emerge from the analyses of the general orientations to the nonprototypical issues. The most common type was the Juxtaposition orientation: the Moral or Normative Model perspectives were juxtaposed with concepts of personal jurisdiction. The judgment that the acts were wrong was in some respects guided by a conception of natural phenomena (or explanations of the "natural" aspects of socially constituted systems, such as laws of social organization); prescriptive statements regarding right or wrong behavior were derived from assumptions about what is natural or normative. Such assumptions took several forms. In some cases, generally stated "laws of nature," or of the supernatural, were invoked as a standard (e.g., "it goes against human nature"; "it violates God's purposes"). In other cases, the act's evaluation as wrong was justified on the grounds that it deviates from biological functions shared by all human beings (e.g., homosexuality is wrong because "human beings evolved to reproduce in sexual relationships"). Assumptions about "normal" social and psychological existence were also advanced by reasoning that engaging in deviant acts would be detrimental to social organization or psychological stability.

Although the judgment involved different categories of standards (biological, social, psychological), in all these responses the categories (*a*) were presumed to represent "natural" systems, (*b*) were used as a standard for comparison, and (*c*) were used to derive prescriptive judgments of right or wrong. Again, in judgments about the nonprototypical acts, we see differences from judgments about moral issues. Whereas the latter were consistently prescriptive, the former were generally juxtaposed with the judgment that the acts are under personal jurisdiction. Thus, for the majority of Group 1 subjects, prescriptive judgments regarding natural states were combined with the judgments that the acts should not be legally prohibited and that individuals should be able to choose for themselves.

It may be speculated that the categories of the natural (e.g., biological) or the normative (e.g., societal) are not perceived as sufficiently compelling to sustain consistent and generalized prescriptions regarding the nonprototypical acts. Consider first that judgments based on deviance from natural states differ from those based on violations of justice or rights. Perhaps this discrepancy is perceived by the individual, leading to a narrower scope of generalization of the negative evaluation. Another reason for the inconsistencies may stem from a recognition that deviations from natural order are not always under the actor's control. Variations from presumed biological or psychological normalcy are often explained as determined by natural forces, and, if the normal and the deviant are both regarded as natural, then the basis for evaluating the deviance negatively may become ambiguous in the subject's mind. There may be a recognition that *deviations* from the natural, which are themselves seen as natural, differ from volitional *trans-*

gressions from the conceived requirements of justice. Our results may, there-fore, indicate that individuals have an intuitive awareness of what philoso-phers term the "naturalistic fallacy."

These possible sources of inconsistencies in judgments would not apply, however, to judgments about abortion, where the juxtapositions were fre-quently between Moral (welfare justifications) and Personal orientations. Insofar as it was assumed that life or personhood originates at conception (see also Smetana, 1982), subjects regarded abortion as wrong because it involves taking a life (though juxtaposing this with a Personal orientation). In this instance, one possible source of the juxtaposition of welfare and personal choice is the ambiguity in defining the origins of life. Insofar as individuals recognize such ambiguity, they may narrow the scope of the generalization of the moral evaluations. A second source may be a perceived conflict between the life of the fetus and that of the mother. In that case, the Juxtaposition orientation would reflect uncoordinated judgments about the need to preserve the welfare of the fetus and the need to uphold the rights of the woman.

The ambiguities in defining the origins of life evident in our subjects' judgments about abortion also appear to be central to the public and judicial debates regarding the issue. Just as our subjects disagreed as to whether abortion is wrong, so do large numbers of American adults as well as judges and legal scholars. The public debates are usually couched in terms of life and rights to privacy and choice. Moreover, many of our subjects, as well as many of the general public, regard abortion as wrong and yet judge that it should be legal and left to an individual's discretion. The elements of public and judicial debates regarding the other nonprototypical issues were also displayed in the judgments of our subjects. The conflicts revolve around the application of fundamental rights of privacy and freedom, around whether the acts are harmful, around ascertaining what is natural or normal behavior, and around the validity of imposing cultural or religious norms and traditions.

At both the public and the individual levels, it appears that abortion, homosexuality, pornography, and incest differ from prototypical domains of reasoning. The initial classification of these issues as nonprototypical was based on our definitions of prototypicality in domains as well as on sugges-tive evidence from survey studies. The present findings provided several indices confirming that, for at least some subjects, these issues are nonproto-typical. Reasoning about these acts was found to differ from reasoning about the prototypical issues, which had been found to form consistent individual patterns of reasoning in many previous studies. Criterion judg-ments about the nonprototypical issues yielded variations in responses to different types of questions (i.e., act evaluation, legal status, contingency, and generalizability), and justifications were distributed across a variety of categories (in contrast with prototypical issues). The analyses of general orientation types showed specific inconsistencies and contradictions in the ways in which subjects typically juxtaposed different aspects or orientations to the issues. (These indices of nonprototypicality apply primarily to the Group 1 subjects since Group 2 subjects were, in the main, consistent across questions.) Moreover, insofar as individuals showed inconsistent patterns, these applied to reasoning about the nonprototypical and not the prototypical issues.

Study 1 still leaves open the question of whether some negative evaluations of the nonprototypical acts might entail consistent judgments since some groups in this society might judge these issues by coherently applied moral criteria. Although this question cannot be addressed in a definitive way without studying many different groups, one possibility is that consistency in negative evaluations and judgments about these acts stems from religious positions. Subjects in Study 1 were selected randomly, without obtaining information regarding their religious affiliations. A second study was therefore undertaken to examine judgments among adolescents from religious schools, obtaining information about their religious affiliation and commitment.

III. STUDY 2: SOCIAL REASONING AND RELIGIOUS AFFILIATION

Groups taking strong stands on the "morality" of the nonprototypical issues might communicate or transmit a strict and consistent position about them in other ways, a position that becomes incorporated into the thinking of the individual members. A group's position could conceivably be that the nonprototypical acts are wrong for reasons of justice, rights, and welfare. Alternatively, the position could be that the acts violate external norms, such as those of the group, or that the acts are sinful, or that the acts violate natural or supernatural order. Such strongly held group positions might produce consistency among as well as within the judgments of individuals. Indeed, strong, categorical positions regarding nonprototypical acts are held and publicly pronounced by the leaders of some religious groups. However, little information exists about how the nonprototypical acts are conceptualized by the members of those groups.

Recently, Nucci (1986, 1989) has conducted research, primarily on prototypical moral acts (e.g., inflicting physical or psychological harm, theft, violation of rights) and religious conventions (e.g., attending mass, receiving communion, women preaching), with samples of Roman Catholics, fundamentalist Christians (Amish-Mennonites from a rural area of Indiana), and Orthodox and Conservative Jews. He found that, among subjects in each religious group, criterion judgments differed by domain. There was also some indication that these religious subjects judge nonprototypical issues (i.e., premarital sex, contraception, homosexuality) differently than they do moral issues.

Nucci's studies were not, however, aimed at in-depth analyses of judgments about the nonprototypical issues. The main purpose of Study 2 was to adapt the procedures of Study 1 to investigate judgments about nonprototypical issues, as compared with judgments about moral issues, among practicing members of a religious group that specifies such acts as wrong. In line with Nucci's research, the subjects in Study 2 were students in Catholic parochial schools. We included only high school subjects since it has been found (Nucci, 1986) that they are more likely to make negative evaluations of nonprototypical acts than college age subjects. The two moral issues (rape and killing) were the same as in Study 1. Personal issues were not included because we wanted to concentrate on comparisons of moral and nonprototypical issues. Furthermore, assessments were made of only three of the four nonprototypical acts in order to generate a larger number of subjects in each cell. Incest was included as one of the items in the study because it had been frequently evaluated as wrong by subjects in Study 1 and abortion and homosexuality because they are most often explicitly specified as wrong by religious groups. The Catholic church, in particular, has been vocal recently in its opposition to these two issues. The church's clear-cut opposition to abortion from the time of conception, it should be noted, has been promoted only since the latter part of the nineteenth century. Prior to that time, it was held that a fetus was not a human being until it was infused with a soul at the time of "animation" (see Tribe, 1990; and Justice Stevens's opinion in *Webster v. Reproductive Health Services*). It was believed that animation, and the presence of a soul, did not occur until 40 days after conception for males and 80 days after conception for females.

SUBJECTS

The subjects in the study were 58 high school seniors from different racial groups (24 males and 34 females, mean age 17-7) attending two Catholic schools (one for males and one for females) in suburban areas of northern California. Participants in the study were chosen as follows. First, a total of 116 students (47 males and 69 females) filled out a questionnaire (taken from Nucci, 1986) pertaining to their religious practices and beliefs. Of those 116 students, 83 (28 males and 55 females) obtained parental consent to participate further in the research. In that group, 70 of the students (24 males and 46 females) were eligible for inclusion in the study because they had stated in the questionnaire that they practiced their religion (most of them had also attended Catholic elementary and middle schools). All 24 males and 34 females chosen randomly from the pool of 46 were included as subjects in the study (given the larger pool of eligible females, more of them than males were included to increase the total numbers). The questionnaire on religious practices and beliefs revealed that the majority of subjects (over two-thirds) attended mass and received communion once a month or more, 96% attended mass at least three times a year, and 87% received communion at least three times a year. Furthermore, almost all the subjects adhered to at least two of the three traditional Catholic beliefs that

TABLE 15

Initial Measure Evaluations (in Percentages), and Distribution
of Subjects by Issue in Study 2

| | Initial Measure Evaluations (%) | | | Subjects Assessed for Each Issue (N) |
Issue	Positive	Negative	"Depends"	
Nonprototypical:				
Homosexuality	36	23	41	19
Abortion	19	14	67	20
Incest	2	95	4	19
Pornography	5	72	23	. . .
Moral:				
Killing	0	97	4	38
Rape	0	100	0	20
Theft	0	78	23	. . .

Mary was a virgin at the time of Christ's birth, that Christ is God and rose
from the dead, and that Peter was the first head of the church.

PROCEDURE, ASSESSMENTS, AND CODING

Each subject was first administered the assessment used for preselection
purposes in Study 1 (excluding only the personal issues that had been in
the preselection for Study 1). In Study 2, however, this assessment was
administered solely to enable a comparison with Study 1 preselection responses, not to select subjects or stimulus items. Table 15, which presents
the percentage of responses on this initial measure, shows that Study 2
subjects, who had been selected for their religious affiliation, responded
similarly to the randomly selected subjects of Study 1; the large majority
evaluated the moral issues negatively, whereas they were divided regarding
all the nonprototypical issues, with the exception of incest. Table 15 also
shows the number of subjects to whom the criterion judgment and justification questions were administered, subsequent to the initial measure. Subjects were randomly assigned to various groupings of two issues, one nonprototypical and one moral. As in Study 1, each subject subsequently
responded to only one exemplar of each issue type, but all three nonprototypical and two moral issues were represented across subjects. For the same
reasons as in Study 1, the nonprototypical issues were presented first. Subjects were individually administered the standard set of questions and
probes to assess criterion judgments and justifications (see Table 2). The
analyses again focused on judgments, justifications, and orientation types,
all of which were coded with the same systems as in Study 1.

RESULTS

Assessments of criterion judgments.—Table 16 presents the findings for each of the standard criterion judgment questions. Chi-square tests revealed no significant differences between males and females in response to either the moral or the nonprototypical issues for act evaluations, legal status in the United States, and legal status in another country. In subsequent analyses, therefore, the data for males and females were combined. We also examined possible differences among the nonprototypical issues (all subjects responded in the same way to the two moral issues). Planned contrasts revealed significant differences among some of these. The issue of incest was evaluated negatively by more subjects (68%) than abortion (25%), $\chi^2(2) = 9.67$, $p < .01$. Subjects were also more likely to judge that incest should be illegal in the United States (47%) than that abortion (10%) or homosexuality (16%) should, $\chi^2(2) = 10.26$, $p < .01$, and $\chi^2(2) = 7.72$, $p < .05$, respectively, and that it should be illegal in another country (32%) than that abortion should (11%), $\chi^2(2) = 9.24$, $p < .01$. Nevertheless, it should be noted that the majority of subjects judged that incest should be legal both in the United States (53%) and in another country (68%).

It can be seen from Table 16 that act evaluations and legal status judgments differed for the moral and nonprototypical issue types.[10] All subjects evaluated the moral acts negatively and judged that they should be illegal in the United States and another country. In contrast, only 41% evaluated the nonprototypical acts negatively, and 73% and 53%, respectively, judged that they should be legal in the United States and in another country. Stuart tests showed that subjects were more likely to give negative evaluations of the moral acts ($z = 9.06$) and positive evaluations of the nonprototypical ones ($z = 7.36$). They were also more likely to judge that the moral acts should be illegal in the United States ($z = 13.61$) and in another country ($z = 17.43$) and that the nonprototypical acts should be legal in the United States ($z = 12.37$) and in another country ($z = 8.24$).

The *contingency* and *generalization* responses of subjects in this study followed the same patterns as for subjects in Study 1. In the first place, nearly all subjects judged the moral acts as noncontingent and generalizable (see Table 16). The number of subjects giving contingent or nongeneralized responses regarding the nonprototypical acts (presented in Table 17) was tallied in the same way as in Study 1 (i.e., those judging that the act should be legal and/or that the act should be illegal but would be all right if it were

[10] Stuart tests showed that responses to each nonprototypical issue differed significantly from responses to the moral domain on each of the three questions. Subjects were more likely to evaluate the moral issues negatively and to judge that the issues in the moral domain should be illegal in the United States and another country.

TABLE 16

Responses (in Percentages) to Criterion Judgment Questions by the Catholic High School Sample of Study 2

Questions	Moral				Nonprototypical			
	Positive	Negative	"Depends"	(N)	Positive	Negative	"Depends"	(N)
Act evaluation	0	100	0	(58)	48	41	10	(58)
Legal status in United States	0	100	0	(58)	73	23	4	(58)
If legal	0	100	0	(57)	7	93	0	(15)
If illegal	...	...	...	...	83	17	0	(42)
If common	0	98	2	(57)	23	77	0	(22)
If uncommon	...	...	...	...	91	9	0	(35)
Legal status in another country	0	100	0	(57)	53	17	29	(58)
If legal	0	98	2	(57)	13	80	7	(15)
If illegal	...	...	...	...	83	18	0	(40)
If common	0	98	2	(57)	14	82	5	(22)
If uncommon	...	...	...	...	97	3	0	(35)

TABLE 17

<small>Percentages of Study 2 Subjects Giving Contingent and Nongeneralized
Responses to Questions Regarding Nonprototypical Acts</small>

	Act Evaluation	
Questions	Negative ($N = 24$)	Depends ($N = 6$)
In the United States:		
Act should be legal	42	100
If legal, act is all right	0	0
If common practice, act is all right	4	0
Total	46	100
In another country:		
Act should be legal	0	0
If legal, act is all right	0	0
If common practice, act is all right	4	0
Total	12	0
Total for United States and another		
country	50	100

Note.—The results for "in another country" include only subjects who did not give contingent and nongeneralized responses to questions framed "in the United States"; in total, contingent and nongeneralized responses to questions concerning "another country" were given by 46% of those who evaluated the act negatively and 67% of those who said it "depends."

legal or common practice). Since some subjects gave "depends" responses for the act evaluations, their data are presented separately from those who gave negative act evaluations. The first column of Table 17 shows that 50% of subjects with initial negative act evaluations judged the nonprototypical acts to be contingent on legal status or nongeneralizable; all giving the "depends" response also gave at least one contingent and nongeneralizable response. In addition to these subjects (18 in all), 28 others evaluated the nonprototypical acts positively. Therefore, 79% (46 of 58) of all the subjects either evaluated the acts positively or gave contingent and nongeneralized responses.

Following procedures used in Study 1, *patterns of criterion judgments* were analyzed in order to determine whether the findings apply to the configuration of judgments of individual subjects. The same four response patterns that were derived from Study 1 subjects' responses concerning act evaluation, legal status, and legal status contingency were evident in the judgments of Study 2 subjects. All the subjects used Pattern A in their responses to the moral domain (i.e., subjects evaluated the act negatively even if it were legal). The most frequent configuration of responses to the nonprototypical issues was Pattern C, with 53% of the subjects falling into that category (i.e., subjects evaluated the act either positively or as "depends," judged that it should be legal, and evaluated it positively even if it were illegal). The next most frequently used configurations for the nonprototypical issues were Patterns D and A, 24% and 18%, respectively (in Pattern D, subjects evaluated the act negatively but judged that it should be legal). Finally, Pattern B was used infrequently (6%) for the nonprototypical acts (i.e., a positive act evaluation in conjunction with the judgment that the act should be legal and a negative evaluation even if the act were illegal; a negative evaluation in conjunction with the judgment that the act should be illegal and a positive evaluation even if the act were legal). Stuart tests (critical value ± 2.79 for α = .05) revealed that Pattern A was used significantly more for the moral than for the nonprototypical issues ($z = 15.43$). Patterns C and D were used significantly more for the nonprototypical issues ($z = 7.57$ and 3.96, respectively).

These findings demonstrate that the results of group analyses of criterion judgments were paralleled by response patterns in individual subjects. Furthermore, the response patterns for each issue type are comparable in the two studies in that the order of frequency of use of the patterns for the nonprototypical issues was the same in Study 2 and Study 1 (combining Groups 1 and 2 as given in Table 9). In each study, Pattern C was the most frequently used, followed by Patterns D, A, and B. Furthermore, in both studies, Pattern A was used by almost all subjects for the moral issues.

Justifications and orientations.—The findings on use of justification categories for the moral and nonprototypical acts are presented in Table 18. The majority of justifications for evaluations in the moral domain were in the categories "justice and rights" and "welfare" along with some use (18%) of the category "deterministic beliefs" (a category not used by Study 1 subjects to justify evaluations of the moral acts). Furthermore, a minority of subjects (28%) used the "authority" category to justify the judgment that the moral acts should be illegal. Subsequent questions (not presented in the table) produced increased frequency of unelaborated responses ("simple disapproval"); the majority of elaborated responses to those questions were in the "justice and rights" and "welfare" categories.

Justifications for the nonprototypical acts were distributed across several categories and generally paralleled the findings of Study 1. The most frequently used category for negative evaluations was "deterministic beliefs" (27%); for positive evaluations it was "personal choice" (38%). The categories "justice and rights" and "welfare" were used infrequently; insofar as they were used at all, it was to justify evaluations of abortion. Negative evaluations of the act of abortion were sometimes justified on the grounds of the rights (18%) and the welfare (7%) of the unborn child. Positive evaluations of abortion were sometimes justified on the grounds of the welfare of the mother (12%). By contrast, positive act evaluations of homosexuality and incest were justified mainly with the "personal choice" category, whereas the majority of negative evaluations were justified with the category "deterministic beliefs."

Table 19 presents the findings for subjects' general orientation types in

TABLE 18

JUSTIFICATION RESPONSES OF STUDY 2 SUBJECTS (in Percentages) FOR THE
MORAL AND NONPROTOTYPICAL ISSUE TYPES

	ISSUE TYPES AND QUESTIONS			
	Moral		Nonprototypical	
CATEGORIES	Act Evaluation	Legal Status in United States	Act Evaluation	Legal Status in United States
Simple approval/ disapproval	0 (16)	0 (27)	2 (4)	11 (16)
Custom and tradition ...	0 (3)	0	0	0
Personal choice	0	0	38 (2)	35
Authority	0 (3)	0 (28)	0	0
Prudence	0 (2)	0	0	0
Welfare	0 (19)	0 (13)	5 (3)	10
Justice and rights	0 (39)	0 (25)	2 (6)	18 (1)
Deterministic beliefs	0 (18)	0 (6)	2 (27)	1 (5)
Uncertain	0	0	0 (8)	0 (2)
Group contingencies	0	0	0 (2)	0
N	57	57	57	55

NOTE.—Justifications for negative evaluations and illegality responses are in parentheses.

TABLE 19

GENERAL ORIENTATION TYPES OF SUBJECTS IN STUDY 2 (in Percentages)
FOR NONPROTOTYPICAL ISSUES

	ISSUE		
ORIENTATIONS	Homosexuality	Abortion	Incest
Type A (Moral)	0	10	0
Type B (Normative Model)	5	0	26
Type C (Consequential)	0	0	0
Type D (Personal)	58	50	26
Type E (Juxtaposition)	39	40	37
Type F (Unelaborated)	0	0	11
N	19	20	18

response to each nonprototypical issue. The Moral orientation (Type A) appeared infrequently and only in reasoning about abortion (the same finding had been obtained in Study 1). Planned pairwise comparisons showed that there were significant differences in orientations between abortion and incest, $\chi^2(4) = 10.71$, $p < .05$; a greater proportion of subjects used the Normative Model orientation (Type B) in reasoning about incest (26%) than about abortion (0%). Also, fewer subjects used the Personal orientation (Type D) for incest (26%) than for abortion (50%); the Juxtaposition orientation (Type E) was used about equally for the two issues. The pairwise comparisons of the distribution of orientations used for abortion and homosexuality revealed no significant differences, $\chi^2(3) = 3.09$. For both issues, subjects used primarily the Type D and Type E orientations. The difference between homosexuality and incest was of borderline significance, $\chi^2(3) = 6.92$, $p < .07$.

The distribution of orientations for these issues corresponds in most respects to the findings of the first study if Groups 1 and 2 in Study 1 are considered jointly. In Study 1, the majority of Group 1 subjects used the Juxtaposition orientation, whereas the majority of those in Group 2 used the Personal orientation. Both orientations were represented in the reasoning of Study 2 subjects. The Normative Order orientation was used to some extent both by Group 1 subjects (14% for homosexuality and 8% for incest) in Study 1 and by subjects in Study 2 (5% for homosexuality and 26% for incest).

ADDITIONAL RESULTS: PERCEPTIONS OF THE POSITION OF THE GROUP

A major purpose of Study 2 was to examine the judgments of participants in a group taking strong positions on the nonprototypical issues. We chose the Catholic church as representative of such a group on the basis of public pronouncements by its leaders as well as of its religious doctrine. It would also be useful to have information regarding our subjects' perceptions of whether the church holds a position regarding these issues and of whether their own positions agree or disagree with that of the church. This type of information was elicited from subjects in Study 2 through an interview given after the completion of the formal testing. We consider here in summary fashion the responses to this follow-up interview insofar as they are relevant to an interpretation of the study's results, noting that these responses could reflect influences of the formal testing that preceded it.

In response to questions as to whether the church takes a position on the issues, all but one of the 58 subjects stated that they believe that their religion considers each of the two moral and three nonprototypical acts as wrong. We also determined that all but one of the subjects agreed with the church's position regarding the moral issues. However, with regard to the nonprototypical acts, 31% agreed with the church's position, 30% disagreed, and 39% stated that it depends on the situation. Furthermore, whereas the majority of subjects said that a person who commits the moral transgressions could not be a "good Catholic," the majority also stated that one could engage in the nonprototypical acts and still be a good Catholic. The differences between the moral and the nonprototypical issues regarding both the extent of agreement and whether one could be a good Catholic were statistically significant (z's ranging from 4.67 to 5.77).

For each issue, subjects were also asked questions pertaining to whether the church could and should change its position. With regard to the moral issues, the large majority (ranging from 91% to 100%) judged (a) that the church could not and should not change its position, (b) that it would be wrong to engage in the acts even if the church's position did change to a positive evaluation or acceptance, and (c) that it would be wrong to commit the acts even in the context of a different religion in some country where they are considered acceptable. In the case of the nonprototypical issues, a significantly greater proportion of subjects (ranging from 40% to 55% on the various questions) than was the case for the moral acts judged that the church's position could be changed, that it would not be wrong to engage in the acts if the church changed its position, and that the acts would not be wrong if acceptable in a different religion elsewhere (z's ranging from 4.03 to 6.71).

DISCUSSION

First, we consider how the follow-up interview informs understanding of the relations between group positions and judgments of its individual members. An interesting feature of those findings is that they demonstrate the varied relations, in each issue type, between individuals' judgments, their perception of the stand of the religious group, and their agreement with the position of the group. Individuals generally perceived that their position on the moral issues corresponds closely with the position of the church, and their estimation of a "good Catholic" was more closely tied to the moral than the nonprototypical acts. Yet the moral acts were judged to be noncontingent in two respects. One is that the acts were judged as wrong *independently* of the position of the church. The second is the judgment that the church could not alter its position regarding the acts. With regard to the nonprototypical issues, individuals did not necessarily perceive a correspondence between their own judgment and the group position (even though they perceived the group to take a stand on these issues). At the same time, the nonprototypical acts were judged to be contingent and nongeneralizable in the religious context to a greater extent than the moral acts were. Consequently, perceived agreement between the positions of a group and its members does not necessarily imply that individuals judge by the authority of the group. Judgments characterized by group contingency and nongeneralizability were associated with nonprototypical acts, about which individuals perceived a fair amount of discrepancy between their own position and that of the group. Judgments characterized by noncontingency to group dictates and generalizability beyond the group were associated with the prototypical moral issues, about which individuals perceived concordance between their own position and that of the group.

The information obtained from the follow-up interview also suggests a mutual and bidirectional relation, rather than a unilateral or unidirectional one, between individual judgments and group positions. Although the moral acts were judged as noncontingent and generalizable, individuals who engaged in the acts were seen to violate standards of a good member of the group (a "good Catholic"). In that sense, good standing in the group is seen as dependent on adherence to noncontingent moral standards. The relation holds in the other direction as well since subjects also judged that the religious group would not and should not change these standards. Moreover, it was thought that, even if the group were to alter its position, individuals would not be justified in committing the acts. It should also be recalled that judgments about the moral acts were justified, not with reasons of group adherence or ideology, but with reasons of justice, rights, and welfare. It can be seen, therefore, that individuals' reasoning about the religious group includes both group dependence and independence. There is group dependence in the sense that moral standards held by the group seem to dictate behavior and the members' standing in the religion. At the same time, judgments about moral issues are not based on group contingencies and are seen to apply to the group independently of positions that might be held by it.

This perspective on morality and religion is consistent with Nucci's (1986, 1989) findings. Nucci found that Roman Catholics, Amish-Mennonites, and Jews judged that acts in the moral domain should not be altered by church authorities and should be generalized beyond the religious group. Nucci also found a mutuality between individual judgments and the group position. Subjects considered proscriptions regarding the moral acts an integral part of the religion that would not and should not be violated, yet they judged that those acts would be wrong even if they were not proscribed by the religion.

The configuration among judgments, justifications, and perceptions about group membership for the nonprototypical acts differed from the configuration for moral acts. Along with disagreements with the church's stance regarding the nonprototypical acts, subjects did not regard good standing in the group to be dependent on adherence to the group's position (i.e., one could commit the nonprototypical acts and still be a good Catholic). However, in another sense, responses to the nonprototypical acts displayed closer group ties than did responses to the moral issues. As already noted, the nonprototypical acts were judged to be contingent and specific to the group to a greater extent than the moral acts. Furthermore, justifications for judgments about the nonprototypical acts were sometimes based on religious or group considerations, whereas justifications for the moral acts were not. Reasoning about the negatively evaluated nonprototypical acts was most frequently based on a normative model, which included conceptions of natural and religious order as determinants of normal functioning. Accordingly, evaluations of the acts as wrong were sometimes based on the perceived deviation from an existing system.

One purpose in studying subjects affiliated with a religious group was to ascertain whether their judgments about the nonprototypical issues revealed a coherence not evident in the thinking of those subjects in Study 1 who evaluated the nonprototypical acts negatively. With regard to the justifications and general orientation types, we wanted to see if the group position would provide individuals with an orientation to a normative or natural order that would not be juxtaposed with the Personal orientation. In both studies, however, most of the subjects evaluating the nonprototypical acts negatively used the Juxtaposition orientation. Using "natural or normative systems" as a standard of comparison, deviations were evaluated as wrong at the same time that the acts were judged to be under personal jurisdiction.

In interpreting Study 1 findings, we suggested that individuals may perceive a difference between their judgments based on justice and rights, on the one hand, and their judgments based on deviations from assumed natural or normative states, on the other. Such a perception might result in a narrower scope of generalization of the negative evaluations of the nonprototypical acts. Insofar as this interpretation is correct, it also applies to the religious subjects of Study 2. Subjects evaluating homosexuality and incest negatively did not use only a Normative Model orientation reflecting a consistent group position. Rather, they too juxtaposed the Normative Model and Personal orientations.

For those evaluating the act negatively, the issue of abortion produced mainly a juxtaposition between Moral and Personal orientations. This finding is also in accord with Study 1. As noted earlier, this particular juxtaposition may stem from ambiguities in conceptions of the origins of life as well as perceived conflicts between the welfare of the fetus and the rights of women to make choices about reproduction.

It is important to keep in mind that a number of subjects in Study 2 did use the Personal orientation by itself. This was unexpected since we assumed that most of these practicing members of the religious group would evaluate the nonprototypical acts negatively and thereby resemble the Group 1 subjects from Study 1. However, the procedure of randomly sampling subjects from a parochial school yielded just about the same division as had been designed for Study 1 with the preselection of subjects evaluating the acts positively and negatively. The fact that subjects in Study 2 were split in their evaluations suggests that controversies and disagreements over the nonprototypical acts are more pervasive than we had originally assumed; even subjects with a religious affiliation and commitment are as divided as the general public. For now, however, this conclusion must be restricted to adolescents from the religious group represented in the study. It may be that members of other religious groups (i.e., fundamentalists) would be more uniform in evaluating the nonprototypical issues negatively.

The similarity between the results of Studies 1 and 2 indicates that participation in a group holding strong positions on a set of issues is not, in itself, the determining factor of an individual's reasoning. Participation in the group may play a role, given the possibility that the Normative Model orientation is influenced by the group position. However, judgments may also be influenced by other groups and individuals holding discrepant views. Furthermore, individuals may very well attempt to make direct judgments about perceived features of the issues (and perhaps even judge the group position in a critical fashion). We would propose that the disputes and ambiguities among the general public, as well as within groups holding strong positions, over the nonprototypical issues revolve around whether the acts (*a*) entail harm to persons or society, (*b*) represent deviations from normal biological, psychological, or societal functioning, and (*c*) constitute expressions of rights and represent realms of personal jurisdiction.

IV. STUDY 3:
THE ROLE OF INFORMATIONAL ASSUMPTIONS

The research on nonprototypical issues that we reported in the preceding chapters examined individuals' judgments without addressing the question of the sources or processes involved in their acquisition. It is likely that public discourse regarding these controversial social issues provides a context for the formation and refinement of individuals' reasoning. However, it is plausible that there may be a bidirectional intersection between public discourse and individual judgments and that individuals therefore not only incorporate orientations given to them at the cultural level but also make inferences based on features of the situations and interpersonal relationships.

The findings of the two studies reported thus far suggest both the relevance of the cultural context to individuals' reasoning and the presence of interactions between individual reasoning and cultural context. It may very well be that the differences obtained in individuals' judgments regarding the nonprototypical issues are partially influenced by parallel differences in attitudes, opinions, and judgments expressed in public discourse at the level of the society at large. However, Study 2 did suggest that such influences may be multifaceted and bidirectional since there were discrepancies between the judgments of individuals and the official stance of their religious group's leadership. It must be kept in mind, however, that members of the group were also exposed to more general public discourse. Such juxtaposition of different types of judgments within individuals' thinking also suggests that they do not incorporate positions given in public discourse in a straightforward fashion. Yet the societal context might influence the formation of the juxtaposition of judgments, given that individuals are exposed to conflicting and strongly maintained positions at the public level.

We must stress that the research that we have conducted to date provides no direct evidence regarding the influences of the societal context. Our research, which was designed to examine the characteristics of individuals' judgments, does indicate that, in addition to the possible influences of public discourse, particular features of the nonprototypical issues may contribute to controversies at the public level, to differences in reasoning among individuals, and to juxtapositions of judgments within individuals. For instance, it may be that some nonprototypical issues present inherent conflicts between differing legitimate claims or rights (e.g., of the mother and fetus in the case of abortion) or between social considerations and salient rights of personal choice (as in homosexuality). Additionally, there may be definitional ambiguities in components of the situation central to the prescriptive judgments. Findings from the first two studies indicate that, with regard to the issue of homosexuality, ambivalence exists about biological and psychological normality in the realm of sexuality. Similarly, with regard to the question of abortion, ambivalence also exists about how to define the beginning of life and/or personhood. Such ambivalence and controversy exist not only in the layperson's thinking but also among experts in relevant disciplines, including biologists, psychologists, ethicists, and legal scholars. For instance, in the early 1970s, the American Psychiatric Association decided not to classify homosexuality as a mental disorder any longer (compare the second and third editions of the *Diagnostic and Statistical Manual of Mental Disorders*—American Psychiatric Association, 1968, and American Psychiatric Association, 1980, respectively). An informative statement of the controversies among politicians, among laypersons, and in the courts over abortion and definitions of life comes from the constitutional scholar Laurence Tribe (1990, p. 3), as put forth in his treatise on abortion:

> No right is more basic than the right to live. And the untimely death of a young child is among life's most awful tragedies. To cause such a death is a great wrong. And if infanticide is wrong, is the destruction of a fetus at eight months of gestation or at five, any different?
>
> Nothing is more devastating than a life without liberty. A life in which one can be forced into parenthood is just such a life. Rape is among the most profound denials of liberty, and compelling a woman to bear a rapist's child is an assault on her humanity. How different is it to force her to remain pregnant and become a mother just because efforts at birth control accidently failed? From her point of view, the pregnancy is also unsought. From the perspective of the fetus, how the pregnancy began surely makes no difference.
>
> If forcing a woman to continue a pregnancy that will almost kill her is impermissible, how different is it to compel her to continue a pregnancy that will probably shorten her life? Or a pregnancy that will leave her life a shambles?

The influence of differing assumptions about social causality and natural or supernatural reality in moral decision making has been stressed in analyses of diversity between cultures (Asch, 1952; Hatch, 1983; Spiro, 1986; Turiel et al., 1987). As an example, Hatch (1983) has pointed out that cultural differences in moral decisions can stem from differences in "factual beliefs." He therefore cautioned against drawing conclusions before disentangling factual beliefs from values or moral concepts: "For the anthropologist to establish the claim about the radical differences in values among the world's populations, they would have to eliminate these differences in factual belief and compare pure moral values uncontaminated by existential ideas" (p. 67). Similarly, Asch (1952) proposed that, to understand variations in moral decisions, it is essential to consider existing beliefs relevant to the situation such as the definition of life (e.g., in cultures practicing infanticide) as well as beliefs regarding natural order and otherworldly events (e.g., in cultures practicing parricide).

Two aspects other than culturally based variations need to be considered in our analyses of reasoning about the nonprototypical issues within this society. First, our findings suggest that evaluations and judgments of the nonprototypical issues are associated with differing assumptions. This was most evident in evaluations of abortion and homosexuality. For example, some assume that life begins at conception and evaluate abortion as wrong on the grounds that it is killing, whereas others assert that life begins at a point after conception (e.g., during the last trimester or at birth) and evaluate abortion as acceptable prior to that point (see esp. Smetana, 1982). These questions are also part of the public debate over abortion (e.g., compare the position taken in *Webster v. Reproductive Health Services*, 1989, which assumes that "the life of each human being begins at conception," with Justice Stevens's assertion in *Thornburgh v. American College of Obstetricians and Gynecologists*, 1986, that "there is a fundamental and well-recognized difference between a fetus and a human being"). A corresponding association may hold for evaluations of homosexuality and assumptions regarding biological or psychological determinants of sexuality.

The second aspect to be considered is that there may be ambiguities in the understanding of these assumptions that contribute to inconsistencies within individuals' judgments. As examples, many who evaluate abortion negatively allow exceptions, most notably in the case of pregnancy due to rape or incest, or give priority to the physical welfare of the mother over the fetus. In turn, those who consider abortion acceptable on the grounds that it is a personal choice because the fetus is not a life also make exceptions based on the reasons motivating the decision to discontinue a pregnancy (e.g., if an abortion were sought merely as a method of birth control or to choose the sex of the child).

These juxtapositions or inconsistencies suggest that there are uncertainties in assumptions about the start of life—uncertainties that do not seem to exist regarding the definition of life after birth, where the injunction against taking a life is usually not qualified. Moreover, after birth, lives are treated as equal, whereas, with regard to abortion, the lives of fetus and mother are often not treated as equal. Uncertainties in the assumption that the fetus is not yet a life, as held by those evaluating abortion positively, may be a source of their judgments that abortion is wrong when sought in lieu of birth control or to choose the sex of a child.

Study 3 was undertaken in order to explore possible uncertainties in the ways in which assumptions are understood and applied in judgments about nonprototypical issues. Two issues, abortion and homosexuality, were used in these investigations because previous findings have pointed to specific assumptions that factor into subjects' judgments and justifications. The expectation was, however, that assumptions would be associated with judgments about abortion in a somewhat different way than they would be with judgments about homosexuality. We hypothesized that particular assumptions about the start of life would be associated with evaluations and judgments about abortion. It was expected that subjects evaluating abortion negatively would generally assume that life begins at conception or early in pregnancy while those evaluating it positively would assume that life begins later in pregnancy or at birth. Nevertheless, it was expected that uncertainties in the assumptions that are made about the start of life will also result in those assumptions being applied inconsistently in different situations.

Our expectations regarding the relation of assumptions to evaluations were less clear cut for homosexuality than for abortion. Assumptions regarding definitions of life have clear moral implications in that most people in this society judge it wrong to take a life. The ambiguities usually center not around the evaluation of the taking of a life but around the definition of when life begins. In the case of homosexuality, we expected that there would be ambiguities in the assumptions about natural or normal sexual functioning and about the evaluative implications of particular assumptions held by the individual. More specifically, we expected to find (a) differences between subjects in assumptions about whether heterosexuality is natural or normal, (b) variations in whether deviations from the natural are considered wrong, even among those assuming that the natural form is heterosexuality, and (c) inconsistencies in the ways in which most subjects apply their assumptions across different situations.

Assessments were first made to ascertain whether particular assumptions are associated with negative or positive evaluations of these issues. Subsequent to the assessment and coding of evaluations, judgments, and assumptions, subjects were presented with descriptions of situations designed to test the consistency with which assumptions are held or applied and their relation to evaluations of the acts; these descriptions are presented below (an example is the situation of a woman who becomes pregnant through rape, given to subjects evaluating abortion negatively). Our expectation was that responses to these stimulus conditions would reveal uncertainties in evaluations of the acts that we expected to be related to ambiguities in subjects' assumptions.

SUBJECTS

The subjects in the study were 87 undergraduates obtained from the subject pool of introductory psychology classes (33 males and 54 females). They were of various ethnic backgrounds and middle-class socioeconomic status and attended a university in northern California.

PROCEDURE, ASSESSMENTS, AND CODING

Graduate student assistants individually administered to subjects a two-part set of questions and probes pertaining either to abortion ($N = 52$) or to homosexuality ($N = 35$); each part was given in separate sessions 1 week apart. Part 1 consisted of a modified version of the set of questions used in Studies 1 and 2 to assess criterion judgments and justifications. In Part 2, counterexamples were presented to test the consistency of the application of assumptions and of their relation to evaluations.

In *Part 1,* the questions were as follows.

1. As in Studies 1 and 2, subjects were first asked to evaluate the act, and their justifications for those evaluations were investigated.

2. Assessments were then made of subjects' assumptions. In the case of abortion, subjects were asked when they considered life to begin; those who had referred to the start of life in their act evaluations were probed so that their position would be stated explicitly. Subjects were also asked why they thought that life begins at the time they stated. They were then asked if there were any exceptions to their evaluations of abortion as acceptable or unacceptable. For assumptions regarding the issue of homosexuality, subjects were asked if they considered it consistent with, or deviant from, normal biological, psychological, or social functioning.

3. Subjects were also posed the following criterion judgment questions (taken from Study 1): (*a*) legal status in the United States; (*b*) law contingency; and (*c*) common/uncommon practice in another country.

Responses were coded for criterion judgments and justifications using the same coding systems as in Study 1. The coding of assumptions, which is presented with the results, was based on responses given by subjects in the current study.

Part 2 was designed to present subjects with counterexamples aimed at revealing additional aspects of the use of assumptions in judgments about homosexuality and abortion. The specific counterexamples were dependent on the evaluations and judgments the subject gave in Part 1. Thus, the counterexample conditions for the second session were assigned to subjects after coding their responses to the assessments in Part 1.

The counterexample conditions for abortion were as follows.

a) Subjects who had evaluated abortion as acceptable and judged that it should be legal were asked to evaluate it when used as a means of choosing the sex of a child. These subjects held the assumption that life begins late in the pregnancy or at birth and, thereby, judged abortion as being a matter of personal choice; even so, it was expected that many of them would judge it to be wrong if used to choose the sex of the child. Judgments that abortion is a matter of personal choice but that it is nevertheless wrong to use it to choose the sex of the child were probed, with the expectation that this juxtaposition reflects uncertainties in the assumption that the fetus is *not* a life.

b) Subjects who had evaluated abortion as wrong and stated that it should be illegal were asked to evaluate it in the case of a woman who becomes pregnant as a consequence of rape. These subjects had assumed that life begins at conception or early in the pregnancy and, thereby, judged abortion to entail the killing of a human life; nevertheless, it was expected that many of them would judge abortion to be acceptable when the pregnancy was the result of rape. Subjects who judged that abortion is wrong because it means taking a life but nevertheless view it as acceptable in the case of rape were further probed to ascertain whether they applied their assumptions consistently. It was expected that the discrepancy in evaluations of abortion would in part reflect uncertainties in assumptions about the start of life.

c) Subjects evaluating abortion as wrong, with the assumption that the fetus is a life, yet judging that it should be legal because it is a matter of personal choice were asked to evaluate the (hypothetical) practice in another culture of considering it acceptable to take the life of a baby up to 2 weeks after birth. It was expected that these subjects would judge taking life after birth as wrong and, in contrast with their stand on abortion, judge that it should not be left to an individual's discretion and that it should be illegal. It was expected that there would be uncertainties in assumptions about the start of life prior to birth.

The counterexample conditions for homosexuality were as follows.

a) Subjects who had evaluated the act as acceptable and judged that it should be legal had assumed either that there is no normative model of natural sexual functioning or that there are multiple forms of natural and/ or normal sexual orientations. As a means of assessing the certainty with which they held these assumptions, those subjects were posed the hypothetically stated case of one's own child being homosexual, and their responses were probed. The purpose of this condition was to highlight the extent to which subjects maintain their assumptions when the connection is made personal.

b) Other subjects had evaluated homosexuality as wrong and judged that it should be legal. These subjects made the assumption that there is a form of normal or natural sexual functioning (and that that form is not homosexuality) but nevertheless regarded the choice to be a matter of personal preference. These subjects were presented with a parallel situation (negative evaluation of an act combined with personal jurisdiction) regarding a different issue—that of theft. They were presented with a hypothetical example of another culture in which stealing is evaluated as wrong and unnatural or abnormal but is not illegal. These parallel situations were used to probe subjects' assumptions about normal sexual functioning further in relation to the judgment that homosexuality should be legal.

Responses to the counterexamples were coded as positive, negative, or "depends" and explanations for the judgments were coded for stated assumptions and/or justifications.

RESULTS AND DISCUSSION

Before we consider the findings regarding subjects' assumptions and their potential ambivalence when they are applied to judgments about abortion and homosexuality, we present the findings on the criterion judgments and justifications. As shown in Tables 20 and 21, subjects in this study reasoned about the nonprototypical issues in ways that were similar to the reasoning of subjects in the previous two studies in that they were divided in their evaluations of each act and that the majority judged that the acts should be legal. A majority of the subjects also evaluated the acts as acceptable even if they were uncommon in another country.

Justifications for the evaluations of the issues also accorded with those obtained in the other two studies (see Table 21). Negative evaluations of abortion were justified by "welfare" responses, while positive evaluations were justified mainly by "personal choice" and "welfare" responses. Negative evaluations of homosexuality were justified mainly by "deterministic beliefs," whereas "personal choice" was the most frequently used category to justify positive evaluations. These patterns of justifications, along with the criterion judgments, paralleled the findings of the other studies. It appears, consequently, that subjects in Study 3 approached the nonprototypical issues in ways corresponding to those of subjects in Studies 1 and 2.

TABLE 20

Responses (in Percentages) to Criterion Judgment Questions for Subjects in Study 3

Questions	Homosexuality				Abortion			
	Positive	Negative	"Depends"	(N)	Positive	Negative	"Depends"	(N)
Act evaluation	57	11	31	(35)	27	35	39	(52)
Legal status in								
United States	94	6	0	(35)	64	19	17	(52)
If legal	0	100	0	(3)	0	100	0	(10)
If illegal	79	21	0	(29)	88	12	0	(42)
If common in another country	50	50	0	(2)	0	100	0	(9)
If uncommon in another country	93	7	0	(28)	93	5	2	(41)

TABLE 21

JUSTIFICATION RESPONSES OF STUDY 3 SUBJECTS (in Percentages)
FOR ACT EVALUATIONS OF HOMOSEXUALITY ($N = 35$)
AND ABORTION ($N = 52$)

Categories	Homosexuality	Abortion
Simple approval/		
disapproval	0	0
	(1)	
Personal choice	50	23
	(1)	
Welfare	16	26
		(44)
Justice and rights	1	0
Deterministic beliefs	21	0
	(9)	(7)

NOTE.—Justifications for negative responses are in parentheses.

Assumptions and Their Inconsistencies

Abortion.—Three assumptions regarding the start of life emerged: that it begins at birth or late in pregnancy, at conception, and at some (unspecified) time during the pregnancy. There was a statistically significant correspondence between these assumptions and subjects' evaluations, $\chi^2(4) = 39.42$, $p < .001$. The first assumption, that life begins at birth or late in pregnancy (e.g., "When the baby is out, after the birth"), was made by 21% of all the subjects. Most of these (10 of 11) evaluated abortion positively. Another 21% made the contrasting assumption that life begins at conception (e.g., "I choose to consider it a human life from conception because there's everything it needs to form a human being. They say that as long as the child is dependent on the mother it couldn't survive. I don't agree with that argument because an infant who is totally normal still depends entirely on its parents"). Most of these subjects (9 of 11) evaluated abortion negatively. Finally, 50% assumed that life begins at some point during the pregnancy. Some of these subjects (10 of the 26) applied this assumption in ways similar to those who assumed that life begins at conception, regarding abortion as wrong subsequent to whatever time during the pregnancy life begins. The others who made this assumption nevertheless regarded abortion as acceptable at any time in the pregnancy. Typically, they regarded abortion as unacceptable for themselves on the grounds that it is taking a life yet asserted that they would not judge it wrong for others (e.g., "If it were me, I think I wouldn't be able to have an abortion after the first 3 months because to me the baby inside would be a living thing and I'd be thinking that the baby could live by itself . . . and it's not a part of me anymore. But I can't really judge for other people; they'll have to decide").

As noted earlier, to examine whether assumptions about the start of life are ambivalently held and differ from assumptions about the status of life after birth, subjects were presented with one of the three counterexamples; those who had evaluated abortion as acceptable and judged that it should be legal (usually with the rationale that it is a matter of personal choice) were asked to evaluate it as a means of choosing the sex of the child. The majority of these subjects (83%, or 25 of 30) shifted in their evaluations in response to this counterexample. Of those, most (22 subjects) said that abortion as a means for choosing sex is wrong but should be legal (the other three subjects judged that it should also be illegal in that case). It appears, therefore, that for these subjects abortion is not consistently regarded as a matter of personal choice. Justifications for the negative evaluations of abortion in the context of the counterexample suggest that the assumption that life begins at birth is held ambivalently. These subjects now emphasized that it is invalid to terminate a pregnancy for the purpose of choosing sex because it ends the life, or potential life, of the fetus.[11]

The opposite effect occurred with subjects who had initially evaluated abortion as wrong and judged that it should be illegal. In response to the counterexample of a woman who becomes pregnant through rape, the majority (7 of 10 subjects) evaluated abortion as acceptable and a matter of personal choice. Three of these seven subjects were unable to articulate reasons for their evaluations; the other four justified the abortion on the grounds that the pregnancy was not the woman's responsibility and that an abortion would alleviate psychological harm to the woman. These subjects' assumption that the fetus is a life appears to be ambivalently held; it is unlikely that the source of a pregnancy, or the psychological harm that it might cause, would be considered sufficient grounds for taking life that is unambiguously defined as present (e.g., after birth).

Finally, subjects who evaluated abortion as wrong but judged that it should be legal because it is a matter of personal choice were presented with the counterexample of a culturally acceptable practice of taking a baby's life within the first 2 weeks after birth (to see whether this type of reasoning was particular to "taking a life" during pregnancy or whether it reflected a more general orientation). These subjects might unambivalently assume that the fetus is a life but also make the judgment that they should not

---

[11] It is possible to shift from a positive to a negative evaluation of abortion as a means of choosing the child's sex for reasons that do not bear on assumptions about the status of life. For instance, abortion under such conditions could be viewed negatively because it would reflect the valuing of one sex over the other. However, all the obtained shifts in evaluations were in fact associated with assumptions about the status of the fetus as a life.

impose their evaluations on others. Alternatively, it may be that the judgment that abortion should be legal reflects uncertainties in the assumption that the fetus is a life. The findings were clear cut in that all 12 subjects presented with this counterexample evaluated the act as wrong and judged that it should be illegal. Also, while these subjects had stated that abortion would be wrong for them because it is taking a life but that they could not impose that judgment on others, they judged a culturally accepted practice of taking the life of a baby as wrong and would impose that judgment on others by making the practice illegal. In response to probes about their judgment in the counterexample, these subjects now distinguished between the "potential life" of the fetus and the "life" of the baby.

Overall, the responses to the three types of counterexamples demonstrate that, for most subjects, the question of when life starts does not have a clear-cut answer: 85% changed their evaluations, and there were no significant differences among those receiving the three counterexamples, $\chi^2(2)$ = 3.86, N.S. Although when life is assumed to begin has a bearing on evaluations of abortion, it appears that such assumptions are maintained with sufficient uncertainty that varying circumstances surrounding the issue (e.g., a pregnancy that is the result of rape, wanting to choose the sex of the child) lead not only to changes in the evaluation of abortion but also to variations in the assumptions about the start of life.

Homosexuality.—The findings revealed more than one association between assumptions of natural sexual functioning and evaluations of homosexuality. Overall, three types of responses emerged. One group of subjects (31%) did not make assumptions of normal or natural sexual orientations and, as expected, regarded homosexuality as mainly a matter of personal preference (9 of 11 of this group).

A second group (34%) made the assumption that different types of sexual orientation are biologically or psychologically determined (e.g., the result of early experience). Since they are determined naturally, both homosexuality and heterosexuality are assumed to be normal forms of behavior (e.g., "I don't see homosexuality as some sort of disorder. I think it's something they are born like that. . . . I just think it's all right because they were born homosexual and they should be able to be like that"). The majority of these subjects also evaluated homosexuality as acceptable (of the 12, 10 evaluated it positively and two as "depends").

The third group of subjects (34%) assumed that only heterosexuality is natural and that deviations from it are thereby abnormal and wrong. The natural, normal state was assumed to be determined by psychology or biology (e.g., "the normal sexual process is for males and females to mate and have offspring. . . . To be homosexual, that isn't a normal sexual drive"; "The most fundamental purpose of having sex is to reproduce") or by religious design ("God created Adam and Eve, so it's not right that only men see men and only women see women because normal to me is just a man and a woman"). Of the 12 subjects in this group, four evaluated it negatively, and seven stated that it "depends" (they evaluated homosexuality as wrong but stated that it is acceptable for others).

A statistically significant association was found between evaluations of homosexuality and the three types of assumptions regarding its possible natural sources. The majority of subjects who did not assume that homosexuality is biologically determined or who assumed multiple biologically or psychologically caused sexual orientations (19 of 23) gave positive evaluations. In contrast, the majority of those assuming one form of normal sexuality (as determined biologically, psychologically, or by religious design) gave negative or "depends" evaluations (11 of 12). A one-sample chi-square test showed that these differences were significant, $\chi^2(4) = 18.84$, $p < .001$.

Here, too, possible ambivalence in assumptions was explored by presenting subjects with counterexamples. Those evaluating homosexuality positively (23 subjects) were presented with the counterexample of the hypothetically stated case of one's own child being homosexual. The majority (92%) manifested a shift in their evaluations in that they regarded the possibility of their own child's homosexuality as undesirable. Accordingly, the judgment that homosexuality is a matter of personal preference was not entirely extended to one's offspring. In most cases, however, the reasons for objecting to homosexuality were pragmatic and personal (e.g., the child would experience difficulties owing to discrimination; it would interfere with family relations and prevent the continuation of the family line). Only four subjects shifted away from their assumptions about the normality of homosexuality in explaining their negative evaluations in response to the counterexample.

The eight subjects who had evaluated homosexuality negatively and judged that it should *not be illegal* (along with making the assumption of the nonnormality of this sexual orientation) were presented with a counterexample containing both these components of their judgment in reference to the issue of stealing (i.e., a culture where stealing is considered wrong, stealing is not illegal, and those who steal are regarded as abnormal). In responding, these subjects first of all did not agree with the legitimacy of the position that stealing should not be illegal (mainly with the justification that it harms others). When the subjects' attention was drawn to their position regarding homosexuality (it is wrong but should be legal) and they were asked if they regarded the two situations as similar or different (and why), all maintained their original positions regarding homosexuality. In contrast with the issue of stealing, where they could not condone the legality of an act considered to be wrong, subjects maintained their position on homosexuality with the justifications that it does not harm others and is, thereby, a matter of personal preference. These particular findings do not serve to clarify the role of assumptions of nonnormality of a sexual orientation, but they do provide further evidence that negative evaluations of homosexuality are based not on considerations of welfare or justice but on an extrinsic standard of biological, psychological, or supernatural normality. In this regard, the findings are consistent with those of Studies 1 and 2.

It is difficult to determine whether assumptions influence evaluations and judgments, or vice versa. It may be, for instance, that the assumptions are ways of supporting existing evaluations. However, we hypothesize that assumptions and evaluations influence each other in a person's efforts at understanding the issues. The findings on homosexuality are unclear in this regard because we did not obtain a simple distinction in evaluations between those who assume a natural (e.g., biological) source of sexual orientations and those who do not. Whereas subjects who attributed homosexuality to personal preference (and not to biological or psychological determinism) evaluated it as acceptable, some who attributed it to a biological source also evaluated it as acceptable. The latter group of subjects assumed that both homosexuality and heterosexuality are biologically determined, without attributing the concept of normality to either one. By contrast, most subjects evaluating homosexuality negatively regarded it as a deviation from the normal. It is important to note, however, that there were distinct and non-random associations between assumptions and evaluations. It is the extent to which assumptions might influence evaluations and evaluations might influence assumptions that is unclear.

The associations between assumptions and evaluations were less straightforward for homosexuality than abortion. Although a relation between assumptions and evaluations of homosexuality was documented, assumptions about the biology or psychology of sexuality were not as central in those evaluations as were assumptions about the start of life in evaluations of abortion. There are two reasons for this difference between the two issues. One is that avoidance of harm to persons is a clearly held moral judgment while maintenance of natural states is not; the second is that social and pragmatic considerations are deemed important in the case of homosexuality. For instance, some subjects evaluated homosexuality negatively in the case of one's own child because they thought that it would result in social hardships or interfere with family lineage. In conjunction with such social and pragmatic considerations, the findings of Study 3 do indicate that there is validity to the proposition that the uncertainty of assumptions plays a role in the types of evaluative judgments our studies of nonprototypical issues have uncovered.

V. GENERAL DISCUSSION

At the outset, we noted the controversial nature of some of the nonprototypical issues. It is abundantly clear from public discourse that, in this society, there are fundamental disagreements among the ways in which people view abortion, homosexuality, and pornography. Accordingly, differences in evaluations of nonprototypical acts emerged in each of the studies we reported here. Study 1 subjects were readily divided into groups that evaluated these acts positively and negatively. In Study 2, the random sample of students with a religious commitment was also divided by positive and negative evaluation, and similar divisions were obtained in Study 3. However, it is not the disagreements or the disputes over these issues that constitute the criterion for classifying them as nonprototypical. Indeed, such disagreements were not apparent in evaluations of incest, which is also not subjected to the types of public debates that exist over the other issues.

FEATURES OF NONPROTOTYPICAL ISSUES

It is the nature of disagreements, insofar as they exist, that is informative with regard to the classification of the issues we investigated as nonprototypical. In the first place, disagreements exist over whether the issues are in the moral realm and should be part of moral discourse. The consequences of the acts are also disputed. Some claim that abortion is killing, whereas others assert that it affects none other than the woman making the decision. Some maintain that pornography is detrimental to the fabric of society, while others regard it as independent of society. We have also seen that differences exist regarding fundamental assumptions associated with these issues, such as when life begins and the biological or psychological nature of sexuality. Although disagreements may be a manifestation of the nonprototypicality of the acts, sources other than nonprototypicality can produce disagreements, and consensus can exist over nonprototypical issues. More central to our definition of nonprototypicality is the existence of conflicting and contradictory judgments associated with uncertainties in assumptions about features of the acts. Consequently, reasoning about these issues is often different from reasoning characteristic of the basic social domains.

The findings of our studies indicate that divisions over the nonprototypical issues are related to the question of personal jurisdiction in important ways. On one side of the debate are the individuals who essentially assimilated the nonprototypical issues into the personal domain. In both Study 1 and Study 2, subjects evaluating the nonprototypical acts positively also judged that they should be legal and maintained their positive evaluations even if those acts were illegal or occurred in contexts where they are not commonly practiced. Indeed, for these subjects, the predominant general orientation to these issues, as assessed by the global analyses, was a personal one. Study 3 revealed that the Personal orientation to abortion was associated with the assumption that the fetus is not yet a life—an assumption, however, that is ambivalently maintained. There were more varied associations between assumptions and the Personal orientation to homosexuality; some made no assumptions about natural sexual functioning, whereas others assumed that different sexual orientations are biologically determined.

In contrast with those emphasizing personal jurisdiction, a less straightforward chain of reasoning is evident among those who evaluated the nonprototypical issues negatively. To state it generally, two broad considerations seem to be at work. One of these is the evaluation of these acts as wrong; the other is a concern with personal choice and jurisdiction. As evinced by criterion judgments and justifications, these two considerations resulted in ambivalent, conflicted, and inconsistent positions. As already discussed in previous chapters, responses to the nonprototypical issues were characterized by criterion judgments of contingency on law and nongeneralizability across contexts, a relatively wide mixture of justification categories, and a juxtaposition of orientations that characterize individuals' overall perspectives on the issues.

Responses to each of the nonprototypical issues included both the combination of negative evaluations and judgments that the acts are out of the jurisdiction of authority and law and the juxtaposition of orientations. However, there were differences among the issues in the forms of those combinations and juxtapositions. A central consideration in subjects' reasoning about abortion was the status of the life of the fetus. Clear-cut assumptions about human life and personhood usually led to judgments that taking a life is wrong in a generalizable way, that it should be illegal, and that it is out of the realm of personal jurisdiction. The fact that abortion is often not judged in this straightforward fashion suggests that assumptions regarding the fetus as a life are ambivalently held. We interpret the findings of Study

3 to indicate that such assumptions constitute a central conceptual problem that partially accounts for the particular configuration of criterion judgments and juxtapositions of justifications that had been documented in Studies 1 and 2.

The other issues we investigated do not implicate a moral feature, such as taking a life, as clearly. In the case of homosexuality (and perhaps pornography), a central conceptual problem for some subjects seemed to lie in how to evaluate deviations from a presumed normative or natural order. On the one hand, they assumed that there exist natural forms of sexuality that dictate what is right. The natural order, which can be based on biology or religion, was regarded by these subjects as being composed of universal and unalterable laws. On the other hand, in applying the notion of natural order, most subjects judged that an issue such as homosexuality should not be legally prohibited since it is a matter of personal choice.

Overall, less variation was found between subjects in their evaluations of incest than of the other nonprototypical acts. (Because the large majority of subjects evaluated incest negatively on the preselection measure of Study 1, fewer Group 2 than Group 1 subjects were questioned about this issue.) The issue of incest among consenting adults, therefore, provides an example of a nonprototypical act over which there is not much disagreement in this society. Of all the nonprototypical issues we investigated, incest was most closely assimilated to reasoning in the moral domain. The majority of Group 1 subjects judged that incest should be illegal in the United States, and they were about evenly divided in judging whether the act is contingent and nongeneralizable. However, a majority of these subjects judged that the act should be legal in another country, and the majority of Study 2 subjects made contingent and nongeneralized judgments concerning incest. Moreover, subjects' justifications in both studies were distributed across categories—as was true of the other nonprototypical issues—with the highest use in the "deterministic beliefs" and "custom or tradition" categories. With regard to incest, the Normative Model orientation was associated with negative evaluations, but a concomitant Personal orientation resulted in judgments that entailed similar conflicts and inconsistencies as the other nonprototypical issues.

CONSISTENCY AND HETEROGENEITY IN SOCIAL JUDGMENTS

It should be stressed that neither conflict nor inconsistency can be seen as characterizing the social judgments of individuals, as a whole. Rather, individuals' reasoning includes patterns of similarity, variation, consistency, and inconsistency, patterns associated with heterogeneity of social thought structured by the different social domains. Similarity and consistency were evident in responses to the prototypical moral issues. First, there was similarity between subjects in their evaluations and conceptualizations of the moral issues. Second, there was internal or within-subject consistency in evaluations, criterion judgments, and justifications of the moral issues.

The similarities between subjects and consistency within subjects were obtained in response to rather clear-cut examples of moral issues (rape and killing) involving unprovoked harm inflicted on others. We used these examples in order to determine whether individuals do make consistent, prescriptive moral judgments (with regard to at least certain issues) alongside other types of judgments (i.e., nonprescriptive judgments and judgments lacking consistency). These comparisons showed that judgments and justifications can differ between issue types even when they are evaluated in the same way (i.e., negative evaluations of moral and nonprototypical issues). The comparison with judgments about issues in the personal domain provided an additional means for ascertaining whether individuals maintain a heterogeneous set of social judgments. For these purposes, we distinguish between inconsistency, which pertains to an individual's discrepant or contradictory judgments about a given issue, and heterogeneity, which refers to an individual's different types of coherent judgments that are associated with different domains. The comparison between responses to moral and personal issues demonstrated an aspect of heterogeneity in social reasoning. Whereas moral issues evoked prescriptive judgments that were considered to apply across contexts, the personal issues evoked an opposing type of judgment; that the acts were permissible and could differ across contexts or in accordance with individual preferences. With regard to moral, but not personal, issues, considerations of justice and welfare were seen to override personal choice and jurisdiction.

Two aspects of the procedures used in assessing judgments about the personal issues provide the context for interpreting these findings. First, the study included personal issues that adolescents and young adults would be likely to recognize as substantive and of some consequence for society and the individual. As noted earlier, previous research has determined that each of the issues (marijuana use, public nudity, and men wearing makeup) fits these criteria. Second, the specific issue presented to a given subject was preselected on the basis of his or her positive evaluations of the act (recall that all respondents to the preselection measure evaluated at least one of the personal issues positively). Accordingly, the results demonstrate that each subject maintains noncontingent, generalizable prescriptive judgments about clear-cut moral issues alongside judgments about the validity of personal choice and jurisdiction with regard to some socially meaningful issues. Therefore, the comparisons of judgments about moral and personal issues provide evidence for the proposition that social reasoning is heterogeneous.

Our interpretation of the findings of the studies reported here, in conjunction with other research, has its basis in the proposition that individuals form differentiated judgments in fundamental domains of social reasoning. These domains, including the moral and the personal, are implicated in reasoning about various issues that do not fall clearly within domains. Given the central role of personal jurisdiction in many subjects' judgments about the nonprototypical issues, an alternative interpretation to the one we have presented is that our findings reflect subjects' accommodation to a central, organizing feature of their culture. That is, the concern with the personal realm in reasoning about what we designate as nonprototypical or personal issues reflects the core "individualism" of the culture (Hogan, 1975; Kessen, 1979; Sampson, 1977), which is manifested in a morality oriented toward individual liberties and personal rights rather than toward duties or communalism (Shweder et al., 1987). From that vantage point, it might be said that the reasoning about personal freedom and choice found in our studies is a manifestation of culturally specific learning and that it would not be found in more traditional, authoritarian, or collectivistic cultures (Shweder, 1986).

Explanations of the process of acquisition and comparisons among cultures are questions beyond our scope here. None of our data bear directly on the acquisition process, and all were obtained solely from one culture (for extensive discussion of these issues, see Turiel, 1989b; Turiel et al., 1987; and Turiel, Smetana, & Killen, in press). Moreover, our samples did not include individuals from groups such as fundamentalist religions, who might judge the nonprototypical issues differently from the religious subjects of our Study 2. It should be recalled, however, that Nucci's (1986) research did show that individuals from fundamentalist groups do make distinctively different moral and conventional judgments.

Nevertheless, the present findings indicate that persons in this culture cannot be appropriately characterized by a single type of social orientation, whether it be the one extreme of individualism or libertarianism or the other of traditionalism or authoritarianism. Whereas subjects in our studies made judgments based on individual freedoms and personal rights, this was by no means their only type of judgment. The clearest expression of judgments based on considerations other than individual freedoms and choices was with regard to the moral issues. We have seen that individuals hold concepts of justice and welfare that they regard as entailing obligations that apply irrespective of personal inclinations and across contexts. These findings are consistent with those of many other studies in which subjects made judgments about a variety of moral issues. As we have already stressed, it is also the case that subjects in the present study did not judge the nonprototypical issues solely with an individualistic orientation. Those judgments were often juxtaposed with negative evaluations of the acts, concerns with cultural or religious expectations, and assumptions about normative natural systems. We also found that subjects who generally evaluated the nonprototypical acts positively did not do so across all situations. A number of subjects in Study 3 shifted from judging abortion and homosexuality on the basis of personal choice in some situations to judging these acts by considerations of welfare or prudence in other situations (e.g., in the case of using abortion to choose the sex of the child). Finally, we note that a body of research on judgments about prototypical conventional issues has shown that another component of social judgments in this society pertains to the coordination of social interactions in social systems, which includes concerns with custom, tradition, rules, and authority (for reviews, see Smetana, 1983; and Turiel, 1983).

HETEROGENEITY OR HOMOGENEITY IN SOCIAL ORIENTATIONS

We return, then, to the proposition that social judgments are heterogeneous, in the sense described above. A variety of different types of social judgments coexist within an individual, including those that could be termed "individualistic," "libertarian," "traditional," "authoritarian," and "collectivistic." This proposition of heterogeneity in social judgments is central to our analysis of nonprototypical issues. Features of social relationships, cultural or social systems, personal concerns, and uncertainties in assumptions associated with the acts can all contribute to reasoning about a particular issue since in constructing judgments about the social world individuals attempt to coordinate different components of their experiences. Our position differs, therefore, from those who propose that individuals' social judgments and actions consist of a central core or orientation that is derived mainly from the predominant organizational system in one's culture. It is the postulate of such a central core that allows for characterizations of societies as organized by homogeneous orientations—for example, traditional, collectivistic, or individualistic (for a critique of such characterizations as one-dimensional stereotypes that fail to account for the plurality of orientations in most cultures, see Turiel, 1989b).

From our perspective, issues like abortion, homosexuality, pornography, and incest are nonprototypical in that they include cross-domain considerations as well as ambiguities in informational assumptions. From the perspective of central core hypotheses, these issues are "prototypical" of norms, mores, or taboos strongly and rigidly held by members of a society. In hypothesizing a central orientation, domain distinctions are not made, and informational assumptions are treated as analytically inseparable from evaluations. Two examples of central core hypotheses, one from a sociological perspective (Gabennesch, 1990) and the other from an anthropological perspective (Shweder, 1990; Shweder et al., 1987), serve to illustrate alternative explanations of our nonprototypical issues. Although Gabennesch and

Shweder propose rather different central cultural orientations, they hold a common view regarding the role of issues like abortion, homosexuality, pornography, and incest in the central orientation that each proposes.

In Gabennesch's position, there is recognition of only one realm of social functioning, that of institutionally contingent and culturally relative conventionality. This assumption is based on Berger and Luckman's (1966) definition of the social construction of reality as consisting of individuals' incorporation or internalization of ready-made social constructions. Berger and Luckman maintained that social practices and institutions have a conventional source (i.e., they are based on shared understandings that become institutionalized and are transmitted across generations) and that such social practices can become reified. They defined "reification" as "the apprehension of human phenomena as if they were things, that is, in non-human or possibly supra-human terms. . . . reification is the apprehension of human activity as if these were something else than human products—such as facts of nature, results of cosmic law, or manifestations of divine will" (Berger & Luckman, 1966, p. 89).

As interpreted by Gabennesch, all social practices are of one kind. They are conventionally constituted and relative human inventions. The only distinction that holds is whether conventional social practices are perceived accurately as such or whether they are reified and, thereby, regarded as nonrelative and due to nonhuman agency (the latter constituting inaccurate, emotionally colored perceptions of social reality). Berger and Luckman's propositions, as well as Gabennesch's translations of them, raise a number of issues that require more precise definitions and analyses (see Helwig et al., 1990). The concept of reification needs to be further defined, as does the distinction that sociologists make between reification and social objectivity or social facts (cf. Durkheim, 1912; Berger & Luckman, 1966, refer to it as "objectivation"). It is also necessary to delineate how individuals construe facts of nature and human products (see Turiel et al., 1987). Furthermore, moral philosophers have traditionally been concerned with what is referred to as "natural law," "natural duties," and "natural rights" (from Plato and Aristotle to Kant and contemporary theorists like Dworkin, 1978; Gewirth, 1978; and Rawls, 1971). These renditions of concepts of natural law, duties, or rights, which are associated with nonconventional and nonrelative moral prescriptions, cannot simply be relegated to inaccurate reification.

Even if it is assumed that all social practices are of human construction, it does not follow that their only accurate characterization is as representing contingent, alterable, and relative conventions. The moral domain is regarded by some to have its source in human rational agency, yet the domain is analyzed as nonrelative and not contingent on particular institutional or social practices (for examples from moral philosophy, see, e.g., Dworkin, 1978; and Gewirth, 1978). The data that we have presented also demonstrate that laypersons typically make nonrelative and noncontingent judgments about moral issues. There is no evidence in these data that subjects were reifying social regulations pertaining to killing or rape. Their judgments were based on conceived obligations dictated by justice, welfare, or rights. How these subjects might construe the origins or sources of the moral concepts is a separate issue. It should be stressed, however, that the subjects did not ground their nonconventionalized judgments about the moral issues in societal, religious, or supernatural sources.

According to Gabennesch, individuals are more likely to reify social practices if society renders it more difficult to see their variability and source in human invention. Consequently, the issues of central focus in our investigations would be considered prime examples of social practices that are likely to be reified by members of society. This is because issues like abortion, homosexuality, pornography, and incest are highly charged and emotionally laden and because transgressions against rules or norms result in strong social sanctions. In other words, the social baggage surrounding these issues is likely to result in erroneous perceptions reflected in their reification instead of in the accurate perception that they are products of localized and variable human activities.

Our findings suggest that dimensions other than accuracy or error in perceptions of human agency are required to explain how individuals think about the nonprototypical issues. It is evident that several elements of social reasoning come together in judgments about these issues. One relevant component is the extent to which the issue is surrounded by strong social sanctions. Since individuals experience the cultural stance, they are likely to take it into account. Our findings indicate, however, that this is only part of the story. It appears that another salient feature of the nonprototypical issues is personal choice and jurisdiction. Accordingly, members of this society attempt to coordinate social norms and personal choice. Interestingly, the prototypical moral issues are also highly charged and entail strong sanctions, but personal choice is not salient. For the moral issues, the cultural stance does not generally pose this type of conflict because the social requirements map onto individuals' judgments of obligation dictated by considerations of welfare, justice, and rights.

In addition to the intersection of domains of judgment, people bring relevant epistemological questions to bear on the nonprototypical issues, questions pertaining to the "nature of things," including the nature of the biological and psychological world. In our view, labeling assumptions about the nature of things "reification" is misleading. The types of assumptions made by our subjects regarding natural phenomena pertained to fundamental questions, such as the origin of life and the biological or psychological basis of sexuality. Indeed, experts have grappled with these issues, sometimes providing explanations in terms of nonhuman agency. Like our subjects, experts do not always have unambiguous answers to these problems and frequently disagree with each other. Our point is not that laypersons and scientists think in the same ways about natural phenomena but that assumptions about natural phenomena are components that need to be taken into account in explaining individuals' conceptualizations of social issues.

Similar considerations hold for an alternative central core hypothesis put forth by Shweder and his colleagues (Shweder, 1986, 1990; Shweder et al., 1987). Unlike the social construction position derived from Berger and Luckman, in Shweder's anthropologically derived proposition judgments based on natural phenomena are not in any sense errors or reified views of reality. According to Shweder, cultures constitute socially constructed realities that are incorporated by their members and that reflect perhaps different but equally valid and objective rationalities. Since the moral order is given in the social order, it is defined by culture; cultures can define the moral order in various ways (see esp. Shweder, 1986; and Shweder et al., 1987). Cultures organized around individualism have a morality that is "rights based" (i.e., the core individualistic orientation), while cultures organized around social hierarchies and social roles have an alternative "duty-based" morality (i.e., the core traditional, authoritarian orientation).

Whereas Gabennesch maintains that all social practices are conventional, Shweder maintains that the concept of convention is a special case restricted to cultures that emphasize a morality of individual freedoms and rights. Within the context of a duty-based morality, all social practices are defined as representative of the moral order of society. In his original formulation, Shweder argued that, in hierarchical, nonindividualistic cultures, morality is conceived as part of the social order. In reaction to a critique by Turiel et al. (1987) of data from India (presented by Shweder et al., 1987), Shweder (1990) has reformulated his categories to include heterogeneity within only the moral realm. In brief, he now proposes that, in hierarchical societies, there are three types of moral "codes" or "discourse": those based on welfare, justice, and rights; those based on social hierarchy and duty; and those based on natural order (including sacredness, tradition, and sin). These are treated as three distinct types of moral argumentation without the possibility of one feeding back on another (however, it can be asked, e.g., what happens when justice conflicts with social hierarchy, particular duties, or the perceived moral requirements of the natural order).

The proposition of a "moral code" based on natural order fails to account for essential components of Turiel et al.'s (1987) reanalysis of Shweder's Indian subjects' judgments of natural phenomena as well as for similar components found in American subjects' judgments of nonprototypical acts. To summarize briefly, it was proposed by Turiel et al. that certain judgments of moral obligation include assumptions about unobservable natural occurrences that entail the possibility of harm occurring to sentient beings. Examples of such assumptions maintained by Hindus from India are the existence of an afterlife, souls of the deceased, and ancestral spirits. In that context, violations of certain norms (e.g., a widow must not eat fish) are judged as wrong because of the harmful consequences. Shweder's reformulation acknowledges only that events implicating assumptions about nonobservable, otherworldly phenomena can be distinguished from other forms of moral judgment. However, a concern with the "laws" of nature is, itself, taken as a moral orientation on the part of the subjects. Shweder's conclusion is premature in the absence of analyses aimed at distinguishing moral concepts from assumptions about natural phenomena. Just as individuals' references to natural phenomena should not simply be relegated to erroneous reification, it should not be assumed simply that they constitute judgments of moral obligation. Rather, assumptions about reality and about antecedent-consequent causal relations must first be disentangled from moral concepts.

Of course, from the anthropologically derived core orientation hypothesis, norms or taboos that are strongly maintained in a society would also be examples par excellence of moral practices in that they are inherent to the social or natural order. Such taboos, which include our nonprototypical issues, would be moral either by virtue of their place in the social order or as stemming from natural order. Our data do not support either of these interpretations of judgments about nonprototypical issues as made by persons in this society. The factors that go into moral, social, and personal judgments are too complex and multifaceted to be mapped directly onto ubiquitous conceptions of social or natural order. Shweder's formulation of a morality based on natural order approximates the Normative Model orientation (see App. A). At least for subjects in our research, such a Normative Model orientation was used infrequently by itself in reasoning about the nonprototypical issues (see Tables 14 and 19); rather, it was usually juxtaposed with judgments of personal jurisdiction (the Personal orientation).

In one sense, our position represents a middle ground between the positions put forth by Gabennesch and by Shweder. Gabennesch treats all social practices as conventional, while Shweder treats most social practices as part of the moral realm because they are part of the social order. Those positions accord a minimal role, if any at all, to domains of social judgment because general, unitary social or cultural orientations are proposed to be the sources of an individual's judgments. Our interactional position takes into account social or cultural contexts. However, it is also based on the proposition that those contexts are not unitary and that individuals make separate inferences about different components of their social interactions, which also reflect their assumptions about the nature of reality.

There is also a question of terminology to be considered. It could be argued that, even granting our interpretation of the nonprototypical issues, the judgments of some individuals should be classified as moral because, in part, they approach these issues prescriptively. We have not chosen this alternative for several reasons. One is that we have used particular terms to differentiate between domains of social judgment, proposing that certain judgments, such as those in the conventional and personal domains, constitute distinct nonmoral categories. In our view, the terms "moral" and "conventional" should not be applied in an encompassing fashion to social reasoning. We believe that it is more precise to restrict "moral" to prototypical judgments and use different terms for judgments that are somewhat different—even if certain issues involve inclusion of prescriptive judgments, it serves the interests of clarity to label them differently. Another reason for using different terms stems from our findings that an individual's reasoning about prototypical moral issues can be distinguished from his or her own reasoning about nonprototypical issues, even though the latter entails prescriptive judgments. Perhaps most important, our terminology reflects a concern with identifying the components of reasoning, as well as assumptions about reality, that form part of social and moral judgments.

Our general position is similar to Asch's (1952) proposition of "relational determination" as well as to views put forth by Duncker (1939) and Hatch (1983). In particular, these and other psychologists and anthropologists have maintained that moral values or concepts need to be distinguished from what has been variously termed "judgments of reality," "existential beliefs," or "situational meanings." As Hatch puts it (1983, p. 67), "Judgments of value are always made against a background of existential or factual beliefs and assumptions, consequently what appears to be a radical difference in values between societies may actually reflect different judgments of reality." This position is illustrated by Hatch with regard to the example of parricide (also used by Asch, Duncker, and the philosopher William Frankena, 1973). Hatch maintained that, where it is practiced, parricide reflects, not a difference with other societies in the value of caring for parents, but differences in assumptions about reality: "Our disagreement is really over the nature of the afterlife. . . . This is a matter of factual belief, not values" (Hatch, 1983, p. 67).

RELATIONAL DETERMINATION: DOMAINS, REALITY ASSUMPTIONS, AND SITUATIONAL MEANINGS

Distinctions between moral concepts and assumptions about reality are also part of Asch's conception of relational determination. Asch cautioned against the then-prevalent analyses of moral and social judgments that merely considered connections between "outer" conditions (e.g., cultural values or practices) and the person's actions. He proposed, instead, that, in addition to externally given cultural conditions and actions, it is necessary to account for the meanings of situations for the actor (including assumptions about reality) as well as for social and moral evaluations and concepts. Moreover, Asch's position was based on the view that the construal of any given situation by the actor includes making assumptions about reality and applying social or moral concepts in ways that take those assumptions into account.

The idea of relational determination is characterized by the recognition that various components may be implicated in social judgments. These include the external or societal conditions, judgments of a social conceptual kind, and assumptions about reality. For these reasons, we consider Asch's propositions especially useful in cultural analyses of social judgment. Moreover, the nonprototypical issues are of special interest for cross-cultural analyses because they provide a context for going beyond the quest for description of similarities and differences between cultures to the examination of the ways in which various components of reasoning are understood and applied in different cultures.

From the perspective of relational determination, it is necessary to identify the different components contributing to individuals' orientations to social issues. As opposed to the proposition that individuals' social judgments reflect an emotive, attitudinal, or conceptual scheme derived from a general cultural orientation, we have attempted to identify differentiated components in reasoning about nonprototypical issues. This is not to deny that a cultural orientation (or orientations) is relevant to such reasoning. It is, however, only one component in the individual's efforts at understanding multifaceted social issues. Features of the situation, assumptions about reality, and domains of social reasoning all need to be considered. Some social events contain elements of ambiguity with regard to assumptions about reality; others are characterized by elements from different prototypical domains. The data presented in this *Monograph* indicate that the issues of abortion, homosexuality, incest, and pornography entail ambiguities in assumptions about reality and are not defined by prototypical domains of reasoning. Along with reasoning about prototypical domains, reasoning about these issues is part of the heterogeneity of individuals' social reasoning.

APPENDIX A

DESCRIPTIONS OF GENERAL ORIENTATION TYPES

TYPE A: MORAL ORIENTATION

The act is regarded as involving a violation of human rights, fairness, or welfare. Subjects employ moral criteria and justifications in evaluating the act. The justifications include statements that the act is potentially harmful to its participants as well as statements that a violation of respect for persons is implicit in the performance of the act. The act is viewed as wrong across all social contexts, and there is the belief that laws should prohibit the act in the United States and other countries.

TYPE B: NORMATIVE MODEL ORIENTATION

The act is judged with reference to a normative model, which is used to derive prescriptive statements concerning the rightness or wrongness of behaviors. Several normative models can be employed to this end, including: (a) a conception of optimal biological functioning; (b) laws of nature; (c) a conceived supernatural order; and (d) the existing social order. Subjects derive "ought" statements from their beliefs about the way the world "is." This orientation generates such statements as, "Because incest is not found in society, it is therefore inherently wrong," "What holds true for nature *should* hold true for human society," and "Because the sexual organs of man and woman are complementary [e.g., in reproduction], only heterosexual relationships are permissible." The prescriptions that subjects derive from whatever normative source they are using are conceptualized as universal and unalterable natural laws applying to human social interaction everywhere.

1. Natural Order

Engaging in the act is believed to violate natural order, go against "human nature," or otherwise breach a naturally given scheme or plan regulating human behavior. Natural order is usually seen as having a genetic or biological origin and may be represented in terms of "laws of nature" carrying prescriptive implications for human conduct. There are two subtypes.

1a. *Genetic or biological determinism.*—The behavior in question is seen either as genetically determined or as constituting a universal biological function shared by all human beings. It is not accepted that genetic or biological variation is possible as a determinant of the behavior. Consequently, because all people share the relevant biological constitution, the behavior governed by this constitution is seen as the only "natural" kind. Moreover, since the subject derives "ought" from "is," any variation on the natural is seen as a violation of a *prescriptive* natural law (e.g., "Since human beings evolved to reproduce in heterosexual relationships, heterosexuality is natural, and homosexuality isn't; therefore, homosexuality is wrong and should not be done").

1b. *Law of nature.*—Both the "natural" and the "should" are inferred by abstraction from nature (e.g., the behavior of animals in the wild). The subject does not invoke particular biological functions (e.g., reproduction) or genetic factors but indicates that nature is a model to be used broadly for deriving prescriptive laws. The "laws of nature" that the subject abstracts are seen as applying to human interaction and dictating ideal human behavior.

2. Religious Order

The act is viewed as wrong because it is sanctioned by religion or because it violates a God-given purpose or does not fit into a supernatural plan regulating proper human behavior (e.g., "God put us on Earth with the instructions, 'Go forth and multiply.' It shouldn't be allowed because it violates this mandate").

3. Societal Order

The existing social order is used to derive prescriptive rules for regulating human behavior. What is found to exist in human society is believed to be what "should" exist. The normative social order is conceived as a prescriptive order. The act is viewed as wrong because it constitutes a violation of the extant social order. Because the act is uncommon and not in evidence, it should be prohibited by law in the United States and other countries. Subjects view the existing social organization as a preferred model for all societies; thereby, variations constitute a violation of ideal social order. It is believed that the existing social order is the best possible one, and the act is therefore viewed as wrong even in societies with a different social organization where the act is permitted by custom or law (e.g., incest is wrong because "it's just not done!").

TYPE C: CONSEQUENTIAL ORIENTATION

It is believed that the act carries with it detrimental effects on social organization or has a bearing on normal psychological functioning. Were the assumed consequences not to occur, then the act would be considered permissible (thus, the act is viewed as wrong only because of its effects). The effects may be regarded either as *inevitable* or *contextual*. If the effects are regarded as inevitable, a consistent response is one that also maintains that the act is wrong across social contexts irrespective of the presence of law or common practice. If the effects are regarded as contextual, then the negative consequences will not always follow the act. Hence, judgments about law and common practice may vary, still maintaining consistency in response.

1. Social Organizational

The act is regarded as wrong because of the consequences that it would have for the existing social organization. It is believed that engaging in the act would lead to such negative social consequences as disorder, chaos, and a breakdown of the social structure (this could include negative effects on such social institutions as the family). Because of these social consequences, the act should be prohibited by law in the United States and in other countries where these consequences are likely to occur. There are two subtypes.

1*a. Inevitable.*—The negative social consequences are seen as inevitable results of engaging in the act, regardless of the social organization of the society in which it occurs.

1*b. Contextual.*—The negative social consequences are viewed as contingent on specific types of social organization (e.g., societies or cultures that have strong taboos or norms sanctioning the act). The subject is able to imagine a society having a different kind of social organization where negative social consequences would not follow from engaging in the act. Thus, these consequences are viewed as resulting from specific kinds of social or psychological organization, not as inherent, inevitable consequences of engaging in the act.

2. Psychological Consequences

The act is regarded as having direct consequences bearing on the actor's psychological well-being and normality. The act is seen as indicative of or leading to psychological dysfunction or abnormality. It is stated that there exists a psychological order that may be disrupted by engaging in certain activities (e.g., incest, homosexuality). Because of these psychological consequences, subjects believe that the act should be prohibited by law in the United States and other countries. There are two subtypes.

2a. *Inevitable.*—The negative psychological consequences are viewed as inevitable results of engaging in the act, regardless of individual differences in personality, attitudes toward the act, etc.

2b. *Contextual.*—The negative psychological consequences are viewed as contingent on specific kinds of individual differences in psychological makeup. For example, it might be believed that incest should be prohibited in the United States because, given that it is such a strong taboo in this culture, people are highly likely to be affected by it in serious, detrimental ways. This belief stems from a conception of the individual as growing up within a culture that prohibits incest and incorporating this taboo into his or her own psychological constitution. Were an individual to grow up in a different culture with no taboo against incest, he or she would have a different psychological makeup and might not be adversely affected. It is stated that there may be psychological variation across cultures with respect to the act in question and that there may be social contexts in which the act would not result in negative psychological consequences for its perpetrators. Thus, the consequences of engaging in the act are not inevitable but contextual.

TYPE D: PERSONAL ORIENTATION

The act is judged positively, and subjects employ personal criteria and justifications in evaluating it. The justifications include statements implying that people are free or should be free to act as they please. The act is viewed as "all right" across all social contexts, and it is maintained that it should be legal and remain under personal jurisdiction in the United States as well as in other countries. Subjects often provide arguments to the effect that having a law against such an act would be arbitrary, not reasonable, or would even imply a violation of personal rights.

TYPE E: JUXTAPOSITION ORIENTATION

The act is viewed as wrong on the basis of the Moral, Normative Model, or Consequential orientations along with the position that the act should not be prohibited or regulated by law because it is an issue of personal jurisdiction and/or *culturally relative*. This orientation thus combines two different types of statements: a negative judgment of the act, based on an orientation of Type A, B, or C, and the lack of prescriptivity of this judgment, as expressed by the personal and/or culturally relativistic statements. In contrast with the other orientations, this orientation does not prescribe for others. The act is viewed as a matter of personal choice and therefore not within the realm of legal prescription. Subjects indicate that there exists a preferred pattern of behavior but that this is a judgment of fact or a value that is not held to be prescriptively binding on human conduct. Variations of this pattern of behavior may be seen as undesirable or less than ideal with respect to a specific purpose, but they are not believed to be violations applying to all human beings. Although subjects in this orientation hold very specific beliefs about ideal or preferred human behavior as reflected in their Type A, B, or C justifications, they do not view deviations from the pattern as moral transgressions. What exists is distinguished from what ought to be, and people are free to deviate from biological, social, or psychological norms. Subjects maintain the act's status as a violation of a preferred pattern of behavior while justifying its status as a matter of personal choice.

TYPE F: UNELABORATED

Subjects make prescriptive judgments concerning the rightness or wrongness of an act but do not provide a moral justification or invoke any particular external model. No further elaboration is given regarding the reasons for their judgments.

APPENDIX B

EXCERPTS FROM SUBJECTS' RESPONSES

The following are excerpts from subjects' responses representing each of the general orientations described in Appendix A. Because of space limitations, only responses to the first few questions are presented (the questions are in italic and responses in roman type). Responses to subsequent questions were consistent with the general orientation.

Type A: Moral Orientation

Issue, Abortion; College Age Subject No. 34

I consider abortion as a form of murder, and I think that a fetus has the right, the ethical moral right to a chance to live, just as much as anyone has a chance to live, and to deny him or her that chance to live simply for the convenience of the mother or the parents as a whole, does not justify the fact that they're killing an unborn child. . . .

Do you think in this country there should be laws against abortion?

That's a more difficult question. I realize that we live in a democracy, and by the very token of democracy one has to give consideration to the will of the majority. And, in this instance, the majority, according to all the latest figures I've seen and the statistics, that an overwhelming majority of Americans, including Catholic Americans, are against an outright ban on abortion. However, I do feel that there should be some sort of laws against it, though as an intelligent person, I know that probably never will happen in this country because of the will of the majority. . . .

Why do you think we should have such laws?

Because I don't like seeing or hearing about unborn children being killed. I'm also against capital punishment, and I think denying someone, anyone, the right to live is the greatest moral mistake anyone can make.

Type B: Normative Model Orientation

Issue, Homosexuality; College Age Subject No. 76

Let's talk about homosexuality. You feel that's not OK. Why?
That would also be for religious reasons, because it's—it's not normal, I guess. I mean it's not like—usually when you think of sexuality, it's just something that seems wrong, I guess. And I've also been brought up thinking that it's wrong.
What do you mean by not normal?
Well, usually when you think of a man and woman sexually—I mean, it just feels like a perversion of that, something that I think is really out of the norm. I guess now, I know it's more accepted. But I still don't think that makes it any more right or wrong.
When you say it's out of the norm, you mean it's not commonly practiced or accepted?
I guess now—I know it's commonly practiced, but . . . I guess I see it in terms of morally right and morally wrong. I see it as something that's wrong, but I know that it is practiced pretty widely, especially now. I guess I see it as something that's sinful, but I don't know if I should elaborate on that. It's just something that's not right.
Any other reasons besides your religious beliefs that make you feel that homosexuality is wrong?
I think—I know it's not really something that I see as being—I guess I'm kind of disgusted by it. That might still be related to my background, but it's not something that I really. . . . When I see it, I'm kind of turned off, I guess.
Do you think there should be a law prohibiting homosexuality in this country?
I don't think it would really help any. I mean I don't think I would really care either way. Because, if there was a law, I think people would still do it in secret, or whatever, so I don't think it would make that much of a difference.
What if it would make something of a difference, if it would cut down on homosexuality; then should there be a law against it?
I think if it changed people's views of it—I guess if a lot of people stopped doing it, it might be because they were afraid of getting in trouble with the law, or something. But I think if it made people realize—if there was a law against it, they might think more about what they're doing and why there's a law against it. I think I might be in favor of it.

Type C: Consequential Orientation

Issue, Incest; College Age Subject No. 45

Incest you said was not OK. Can you tell me why you say that?

Genetic reasons, moral reasons. There's a sanctity to the family as well as the obligation to society. And, in doing so, I think you could cause an imbalance in people.

So when you say "genetic," you mean because they could have children who were not normal?

Yeah, because improper elements of genetics do arise.

How about people who are either using contraception or agreed to be sterilized to make sure they didn't have any children. What would you think about something like that?

In incest? I still think it's wrong, just because the family, nuclear or extended to a certain extent—twelfth cousin, or whatever—it's still harmful to the family as a unit. A family grows, but a relationship unites, and a family develops. And you can't have uniting and developing in one. You can only have parts joined together, as in the family tree. . . . A family is one unit, whether it's mother, father, children, grandchildren, cousins, and each one has—except the mother and father who have already united—each one has an opportunity to unite with somebody else. But doing it within the family is—it just doesn't make sense. If there's no growth in that, there's nothing to come from that, no additions or anything.

Do you think there should be laws in this country against incest?

Yes, there are laws, and I agree with them. For protection of society, to make sure that if we are going to grow, that we grow naturally and through nature, and not have it, through our knowledge, have it interrupted in a way that can cause harm to offspring.

So, if we're talking about incest where there won't be any children from the couple, do you still think it should be illegal?

It should be illegal. It's also immoral, in my opinion.

Issue, Pornography; College Age Subject No. 59

I think it hurts people, mentally and psychologically.

In what way does it hurt people? How does it hurt them psychologically?

OK, whenever they read all the dirty magazines or see all the movies—OK, watching the movies is escapism. You totally put yourself into the movie, mostly. And since you are so concentrated—even after the actual movie is over, and you may constantly recall what you have seen. And I don't think it's a good thing to do.

You said it might cause you to recall, constantly, or to become obsessed with what you've seen in the movies. What's wrong with that?

They tend to do, you know, all the rapes are caused by all these movies, according to a survey.

What if there were no connection between someone viewing pornography and going out and committing rape?

It has to do with morality. Even if something is legal, it might be immoral to me. . . . It's not healthy. It's not healthy at all.

In what way is it not healthy?

Both mentally and physically. The ones who act in this kind of movie, they're just depreciating their personality. Even the producers of these kinds of movies are not in the right attitude. They don't have the right attitude. They just want to earn money from people being lustful.

Why does pornography depreciate someone's personality? How is it psychologically harmful?

Well, it just robs away people's privacy. It's something between two people, and it's very private. People tend to hurt people's privacy by making a movie so that people can enjoy it—so called enjoy it. And I don't think it's right.

Do you think there should be a law that prohibits the reading or viewing of pornographic literature in this country?

I think so, but it's impossible. It's a free country.

But you think there should be a law prohibiting it?

Don't we have a law now?

I guess it varies from area to area.

It's too lenient.

Why should there be a law prohibiting pornography?

Because it's not right to do it. . . .

Type D: Personal Orientation

Issue, Incest; College Age Subject No. 85

If we're talking about two consenting adults, I think anything goes. I think it's a private affair. That's it.

Do you think the law should allow incest in this country?

I wasn't aware that there was actually a law against incest among consenting adults. Is there? . . . There probably is a law. I would prefer to see an absence of laws on the subject, insofar as adults are concerned.

Why do you think there should be no laws then?

Well, I don't think there should be a law. I don't believe in an excessive law, I guess. I guess I'm thinking of a law that would legalize the situation, saying it was OK to do such and such. I would rather there be an absence of any statement on the subject.

Issue, Abortion; High School Age Subject No. 53

Well, I think abortion is something that should completely be the woman's own decision. I mean, I don't think it's something that I could handle going through, but I think it definitely should be left as a decision of the pregnant woman. I don't think that it should be decided by anything or anyone else. . . . It seems to me more like it's a medical issue, rather than a moral issue. And it would work better if it were looked at that way.

So do you think that there should be a law that allows abortion in this country?

Yes.

And why do you think that?

Because I think that it should be a decision of the mother and it shouldn't be against the law. And also, if it were against the law, people who were desperate would have an abortion illegally, and that can only lead to serious problems.

What sort of problems could it lead to?

Well, like in the sixties when they had all the illegal clinics that weren't sanitary and also the people with coat hangers, in desperation, who couldn't afford to go to the illegal clinics.

Can you think of any special circumstances where you think an abortion might not be justified?

Not really, because it's justified by the decision of the woman to have one, whatever her reasons may be.

So you think that any reason she might have would be a good reason? Or that you don't even have to judge the reason?

No, you don't have to, I mean, just because this woman decided that that's what she wanted to do is enough.

Type E: Juxtaposition Orientation

Issue, Homosexuality; High School Age Subject No. 44

You said that it was not all right for people to engage in homosexuality. Can you tell me why you think it is not all right?

Well, um, for religious reasons. I'm a Christian, and I believe that the Bible is real specific in saying that it's wrong. I'm aware of the fact that there are homosexuals and have feelings about that and about, you know, different ideas on, I really believe in, that we were created not to be homosexual and that to a certain extent we choose to engage in sexual acts that way and, but at the same time I really would defend someone's right to express their sexuality that way.

Well, what is wrong about homosexuality according to the Bible?

Well, it talks about it being, I'm not sure exactly what the terminology is, but I think it talks about it basically being, uh, immoral, being, uh, evil.

But at the same time you would defend someone's right to commit an immoral or evil act?

I would because I think that we live in a society where there's a lot of evil and we can't start, I mean that's my feeling that it is evil, but I would still defend someone's right to practice that in the privacy of their own, you know. I know a lot of parents that wouldn't want their children to be in a classroom that was taught by someone who they suspected to be homosexual, and I feel like that really doesn't affect their ability to be a good teacher, and so, in that sense, I would defend their right to practice that. I think there are a lot of things that are wrong in the society that people engage in, and we don't, you know, we can't start trying to, as a group of people, deciding what's right and what's wrong. I'm entitled to my feelings, but someone else is equally entitled to theirs.

Do you think there should be a law against homosexuality in this country?

No, I don't. That's what I'm saying. I think there would be no way to try and segregate, you know, the "good people" from the "bad people," and who would decide that. That whole issue scares me, and I wouldn't want to try and do that.

Why does it scare you?

Because I feel like we live in a society where a lot of people have very different feelings on what's right and wrong, and the Moral Majority, for example, is one group who would love to make laws on all of what they believe is right, and that scares me to death because I don't want them doing that. I don't agree with a lot of what they say, and to have, for it come to law that the way that they want things to become law I don't know who would be capable of making those decisions for everyone, so that's what scares me, and that's why I wouldn't want that to happen because I don't think anybody is really qualified to make those kind of decisions for everyone.

Issue, Pornography; College Age Subject No. 102

I think that pornography as opposed to art which involves explicit sex or something like that and the line is very fine, I think that it's really in the eye of the beholder, whether you're partaking of an artistic, whether you're appreciating art or you're having a pornographic experience. And as far as a pornographic experience I think that's a degradation of the human sexual drive. I mean that's not the proper way to. . . .

How is it a degradation? In what way does it degrade people?

Well, it's um, I have to answer that on a religious basis. I think that sex is something that God meant for a man and wife, for a husband and wife, and anything short of that ideal is something short of the ideal. And pornography is just sort of a quick fix to . . . it's just like eating candy if you're hungry. It's not particularly good for you. It doesn't really satisfy the craving, it just makes it go away for awhile. That's what you think you want.

Well, what's wrong with that? What's wrong with pornography in the same way that eating candy is wrong?

Well, let's see if I can spontaneously carry out my analogy. I think that eating candy is not good for your system to eat candy to make yourself not hungry, and that also means that you're not going to be hungry for the proper kind of food that you need for health. And, in the same way, sex is meant, it has its place and everything, and if you get it all skewed up, cause it's a bad thing, cause it's a very good analogy to candy actually. It's not, it's gonna mess up a relationship you have with a spouse, or will have.

Will it always destroy a relationship?

It wouldn't always destroy it, but it would certainly weaken it I would think. Of course I can't speak from experience.

How would it weaken the relationship?

Well, the um, you know it's a very exclusive relationship, just two, and it's not something that's shared with someone else or not the kind of thing you run after by yourself or anything, so it disassociates the sexual satisfaction from the proper sexual satisfier. . . .

What if one weren't married, say, and was viewing pornography? Is there something wrong with that?

Yes, I would say, I would definitely say so. I'm having trouble defining exactly why. I think first of all because it, it tends to lead to larger and larger problems and can get carried away, and, second of all, it weakens a future relationship in that you've got, you go into it, and you go into it disassociated. You've already got previous sexual gratification experiences that are unrelated to your spouse.

What's wrong with having outside sources? Outside gratification?

Well, again, as I see it, God meant for sex to be entirely within marriage and not outside. And that's how he designed the relationship to work.

OK. Do you think there should be a law that prohibits the reading of pornographic literature in this country?

No. I think that one of the important things about this country is that there is that freedom, and once you start clamping anybody's religious views, even your own, on anything, you get everything messed up and religious freedom goes out the window, for everyone, including the people whose religion is imposed on the masses. So, and also, I do think that the difference between the pornographic response and the artistic response is in the beholder, and well, I think that there's less potential for artistic response in certain works, but you can't, I don't think the government, I don't think that's in line with the Constitution and the intent of this country to make that law.

REFERENCES

American Psychiatric Association. (1968). *Diagnostic and statistical manual of mental disorders.* 2d ed. Washington, D.C.: American Psychiatric Press.

American Psychiatric Association. (1980). *Diagnostic and statistical manual of mental disorders.* 3d ed. Washington, D.C.: American Psychiatric Press.

Asch, S. E. (1952). *Social psychology.* Englewood Cliffs, NJ: Prentice-Hall.

Berger, P. L., & Luckman, T. (1966). *The social construction of reality: A treatise in the sociology of knowledge.* New York: Doubleday.

Berkowitz, M. W., Guerra, N., & Nucci, L. (in press). Sociomoral development and drug and alcohol abuse. In W. M. Kurtines & J. G. Gewirtz (Eds.), *Handbook of moral behavior and development* (Vol. 1). Hillsdale, NJ: Erlbaum.

Bowers v. Hardwick, 478 U.S. 196, 1986.

Chomsky, N. (1980). On cognitive structures and their development. In M. Piatelli-Palmarini (Ed.), *Language and learning: The debate between Jean Piaget and Noam Chomsky* (pp. 35–54). Cambridge, MA: Harvard University Press.

Cohen, J. (1960). A coefficient of agreement for nominal scales. *Educational and Psychological Measurement,* **20,** 37–46.

Davidson, P., Turiel, E., & Black, A. (1983). The effect of stimulus familiarity on the use of criteria and justifications in children's social reasoning. *British Journal of Developmental Psychology,* **1,** 49–65.

Duncan, B. (1986). *The coordination of moral and social conventional knowledge: A developmental analysis of children's understandings of multifaceted social stories.* Unpublished doctoral dissertation, University of California, Berkeley.

Duncker, K. (1939). Ethical relativity? (An inquiry into the psychology of ethics). *Mind,* **48,** 39–53.

Durkheim, E. (1965). *The elementary forms of the religious life.* New York: Free Press. (Original work published 1912)

Dworkin, R. (1978). *Taking rights seriously.* Cambridge, MA: Harvard University Press.

Fodor, J. (1983). *The modularity of mind.* Cambridge, MA: MIT/Bradford Press.

Frankena, W. (1973). *Ethics.* Englewood Cliffs, NJ: Prentice-Hall.

Gabennesch, H. (1990). The perception of social conventionality by children and adults. *Child Development,* **61,** 2047–2059.

Gewirth, A. (1978). *Reason and morality.* Chicago: University of Chicago Press.

Gilligan, C. (1977). In a different voice: Women's conceptions of self and of morality. *Harvard Educational Review,* **47,** 481–517.

Gilligan, C., Kohlberg, L., Lerner, J., & Belenky, M. (1970). *Moral reasoning about sexual dilemmas: The development of an interview and scoring system.* Unpublished manuscript, Harvard University.

Goodman, L. A. (1972). A modified multiple regression approach to the analysis of dichotomous variables. *American Sociological Review, 37,* 28–46.

Harris, L., & Westin, A. F. (1979). *The dimensions of privacy: The National Opinion Research Survey of Attitudes toward Privacy.* Steven's Point, WI: Century Insurance.

Hatch, E. (1983). *Culture and morality: The relativity of values in anthropology.* New York: Columbia University Press.

Helwig, C. C., Tisak, M., & Turiel, E. (1990). Children's social reasoning in context. *Child Development, 61,* 2068–2078.

Hogan, R. (1975). Theoretical egocentrism and the problem of compliance. *American Psychologist, 30,* 533–539.

Jancaterino, W. S. (1982). *The relationship between children's understanding of social influence and their moral evaluation of harm.* Unpublished doctoral dissertation, University of California, Santa Cruz.

Kessen, W. (1979). The American child and other cultural inventions. *American Psychologist, 34,* 815–820.

Killen, M. (1990). Children's evaluations of morality in the context of peer, teacher-child, and family relations. *Journal of Genetic Psychology, 151,* 395–410.

Killen, M., Leviton, M., & Cahill, J. (1989). *Adolescent reasoning about drug use.* Unpublished manuscript, Wesleyan University.

Kohlberg, L. (1969). Stage and sequence: The cognitive-developmental approach to socialization. In D. Goslin (Ed.), *Handbook of socialization theory and research* (pp. 347–480). Chicago: Rand-McNally.

Magidson, J. (1978). An illustrative comparison of Goodman's approach to logit analysis with dummy variable regression analysis. In J. Magidson (Ed.), *Analyzing qualitative/ categorical data: Log-linear models and latent structure analysis* (pp. 27–54). New York: University Press of America.

Marascuilo, L. A., & Busk, P. E. (1987). Log-linear models: A way to study main effects and interaction for multidimensional contingency tables with categorical data. *Journal of Counseling Psychology, 34,* 443–455.

McClosky, H., & Brill, A. (1983). *Dimensions of tolerance: What Americans believe about civil liberties.* New York: Russell Sage.

Miller, J. G., & Bersoff, D. M. (1988). When do American children and adults reason in social conventional terms? *Developmental Psychology, 24,* 366–375.

Nucci, L. P. (1981). The development of personal concepts: A domain distinct from moral or social concepts. *Child Development, 52,* 114–121.

Nucci, L. P. (1986). Children's conceptions of morality, societal convention, and religious prescription. In C. Harding (Ed.), *Moral dilemmas: Philosophical and psychological reconsiderations of the development of moral reasoning* (pp. 138–174). Chicago: Precedent.

Nucci, L. P. (1989). *God's word, religious rules and their relation to Christian and Jewish children's concepts of morality.* Paper presented at the biennial meeting of the Society for Research in Child Development, Kansas City, MO.

Nucci, L., Guerra, N., & Lee, J. (1989). *Moral, personal, prudential, and normative aspects of adolescent drug use.* Paper presented at the biennial meeting of the Society for Research in Child Development, Kansas City, MO.

Piaget, J. (1932). *The moral judgment of the child.* London: Routledge & Kegan Paul.

Rawls, J. (1971). *A theory of justice.* Cambridge, MA: Harvard University Press.

Roe v. Wade, 410 U.S. 113, 1973.

Roth v. United States, 354 U.S. 476, 1957.

Sampson, E. E. (1977). Psychology and the American ideal. *Journal of Personality and Social Psychology,* **35,** 767–782.

Searle, J. (1983, October 27). The world turned upside down. *New York Review of Books,* pp. 74–79.

Shweder, R. A. (1986). Divergent rationalities. In D. W. Fiske & R. A. Shweder (Eds.), *Metatheory in social science: Pluralisms and subjectivities* (pp. 163–196). Chicago: University of Chicago Press.

Shweder, R. A. (1990). In defense of moral realism. *Child Development,* **61,** 2060–2067.

Shweder, R. A., Mahapatra, M., & Miller, J. G. (1987). Culture and moral development. In J. Kagan & S. Lamb (Eds.), *The emergence of morality in young children* (pp. 1–83). Chicago: University of Chicago Press.

Smetana, J. G. (1982). *Concepts of self and morality: Women's reasoning about abortion.* New York: Praeger.

Smetana, J. G. (1983). Social-cognitive development: Domain distinctions and coordinations. *Developmental Review,* **3,** 131–147.

Smetana, J. G. (1988). Adolescents' and parents' conceptions of parental authority. *Child Development,* **59,** 321–335.

Spiro, M. (1986). Cultural relativism and the future of anthropology. *Cultural Anthropology,* **1,** 259–286.

Stoddart, T., & Turiel, E. (1985). Children's concepts of cross-gender activities. *Child Development,* **56,** 1241–1252.

Thornburgh v. American College of Obstetricians and Gynecologists, 476 U.S. 747, 1986.

Tribe, L. H. (1990). *Abortion: The clash of absolutes.* New York: Norton.

Turiel, E. (1978). The development of concepts of social structure: Social convention. In J. Glick & A. Clarke-Stewart (Eds.), *The development of social understanding* (pp. 25–107). New York: Gardner.

Turiel, E. (1983). *The development of social knowledge: Morality and convention.* Cambridge: Cambridge University Press.

Turiel, E. (1989a). Domain-specific social judgments and domain ambiguities. *Merrill-Palmer Quarterly,* **35,** 89–114.

Turiel, E. (1989b). The social construction of social construction. In W. Damon (Ed.), *Child development today and tomorrow* (pp. 86–106). San Francisco: Jossey-Bass.

Turiel, E., & Davidson, P. (1986). Heterogeneity, inconsistency, and asynchrony in the development of cognitive structures. In I. Levin (Ed.), *Stage and structure: Reopening the debate* (pp. 106–143). Norwood, NJ: Ablex.

Turiel, E., Killen, M., & Helwig, C. C. (1987). Morality: Its structure, functions, and vagaries. In J. Kagan & S. Lamb (Eds.), *The emergence of moral concepts in young children* (pp. 155–244). Chicago: University of Chicago Press.

Turiel, E., & Smetana, J. (1984). Social knowledge and action: The coordination of domains. In W. M. Kurtines & J. L. Gewirtz (Eds.), *Morality, moral behavior, and moral development: Basic issues in theory and research* (pp. 261–282). New York: Wiley.

Turiel, E., Smetana, J. G., & Killen, M. (in press). Social contexts in social cognitive development. In W. M. Kurtines & J. L. Gewirtz (Eds.), *Handbook of moral behavior and development: Vol. 2. Research* (pp. 307–309). Hillsdale, NJ: Erlbaum.

Webster v. Reproductive Health Services, 109 S.Ct. 3040, 1989.

Zwick, R., Neuhoff, V., Marascuilo, L. A., & Levin, J. R. (1982). Statistical tests for correlated proportions: Some extensions. *Psychological Bulletin,* **92,** 258–271.

ACKNOWLEDGMENTS

We are grateful for the cooperation of the subjects, teachers, and administrators at the following high schools: Alameda, Oakland, St. Mary's, and Holy Names. Thanks are due to Lyda Beardsley, Sara Brose, Batya Friedman, Peter Kahn, Marta Laupa, Terry Madden, and Gary Yabrove, who assisted in the research. We also wish to acknowledge the valuable comments on earlier drafts of the manuscript given to us by Sara Brose, Charles Helwig, Melanie Killen, Judith Smetana, and Mark Spranca. Carolyn Hildebrandt was supported by a National Research Service Award (HD 07181) for postdoctoral research in the Developmental Psychology Training Program, University of California, Berkeley.

Correspondence should be addressed to Elliot Turiel, Graduate School of Education, University of California, Berkeley, CA 94720.

COMMENTARY

WHY ARE NONPROTOTYPICAL EVENTS SO DIFFICULT, AND WHAT ARE THE IMPLICATIONS FOR SOCIAL-DEVELOPMENTAL PSYCHOLOGY?

HERBERT D. SALTZSTEIN

Prior to the rise of the cognitive structural approach to moral development, little thought was given to the specific nature of moral issues in psychological research. Moral judgment was treated as just another kind of social judgment, different not in kind but only perhaps in degree of the person's commitment. This assumption characterized research motivated by psychodynamic theories and especially behavioristic research, whether of the conditioning (e.g., Aronfreed, 1968) or social learning (e.g., Bandura & Walters, 1963) variety.

It was one of Kohlberg's most important contributions to the psychological study of morality to insist on differentiating moral issues from other social issues. He pointed out that moral judgments had certain defining characteristics that distinguished them from other kinds of value judgments. Among their essential characteristics were two: moral judgments took (i.e., should take) precedence over other kinds of judgments (e.g., aesthetic, prudential), and they were universal, that is, obligatory for all participants once the situation is understood from all their points of view. The latter, of course, places Kohlberg's approach squarely within the Kantian and neo-Kantian (e.g., Rawls, 1971) tradition.

In a series of ground-breaking studies, Turiel and his colleagues (e.g., Turiel, 1983) further differentiated the domain—one might say, refined the core—of morality. Specifically, they distinguished among three kinds of

I would like to thank Dr. David Bearison for critically reading an earlier version of this Commentary.

value judgments and thought: the *moral* (universal, noncontingent, and based ultimately on the welfare of others); the *conventional* (nonuniversal, contingent, and based on concern for preserving social organization); and the *personal* (also nonuniversal and contingent but based on the different concern or principle of personal agency).

This *Monograph* by Turiel, Hildebrandt, and Wainryb is in keeping with the tradition of viewing development as a process of differentiation and integration (Werner, 1948)—in a very special sense. One of the major conclusions made by Turiel and his colleagues in this and in their past research is that the moral, conventional, and personal domains do not emerge from an undifferentiated mass, as was previously assumed, but appear at a very early age, as early as measurement is feasible (although they are not innate). Therefore, the domains themselves do not seem to emerge by means of a series of differentiations, but Turiel et al.'s theory and research demonstrate how the study of social-moral cognition develops through a series of differentiations. Thus, historically, the moral was initially not distinguished in principle from the nonmoral; then Kohlberg and others showed how moral cognition had to be differentiated from other cognition in order to discover its developmental course. Now Turiel and his coworkers have shown how moral cognition must be further differentiated from other evaluative domains, such as the social-conventional, personal, and psychological, in order to further our understanding of their development.

In this *Monograph*, Turiel et al. have turned their attention to those nonprototypical issues that appear to span domains, or at least do not fit neatly within any one domain. Perhaps it is not surprising that, with one exception (incest), these issues also turn out to be highly controversial and, in at least one case (abortion), extremely socially divisive. Thus, the purpose of these studies is to investigate why judgments of these issues are so difficult, divisive, and controversial and what accounts for interpersonal differences in judgment. Phrased another way, what makes an issue nonprototypical?

Rather than wielding a sharp analytic scalpel as a philosopher might (e.g., Kant, 1964/1785) or applying an earpiece to detect subtle differences in social functions as a sociologist or an anthropologist might (e.g., Durkheim, 1961/1925), Turiel, Hildebrandt, and Wainryb have carefully examined the judgment and reasoning that ordinary reasoners apply to these nonprototypical issues and how these differ as compared with that applied to moral and personal issues. Less developmentally and cognitively oriented investigators might have used a more standard quantitative method, such as factor analysis, in their investigations. Instead, and I think correctly, Turiel et al. have carefully examined both the (criterion) judgments and (justifying) reasons. In my view, this is the empirical analogue of the analytic (philosophical) method.

By raising these issues, the investigations pose fundamental questions concerning the organization and functioning of moral thought in relation to other forms of social thought. Let us consider some possible answers to these questions.

1. Issues like abortion and pornography might lie squarely within the category of moral issues but be of a specially difficult kind where different moral principles clash and lead to different judgments. Perhaps basic moral principles, such as deontological and utilitarian (e.g., Frankena, 1973), are both applicable, resulting in conflict on these issues. For example, abortion might violate the rights of the unborn, but it may also benefit society by restricting population growth and assuring better resources for those infants who are born.[1] In sum, while prototypical issues may be judged by the application of lower-level moral rules, nonprototypical issues require higher-level moral principles.

2. A variation of the above is the proposition that, because these nonprototypical issues are moral issues of greater cognitive complexity, what we see as domain differences are really manifestations of a *décalage* in judgment. By analogy, nonprototypical issues are to prototypical issues what conservation of volume is to conservation of matter.[2]

3. Nonprototypical issues might be ambiguous as to their proper category, that is, the moral, the conventional, or the personal. This ambiguity might be revealed in heterogeneity across persons and/or variation across situations or occasions within persons. In either case, the critical point is that, once a category decision is made, the judgments and reasoning follow predictably. On this view, it is for the reasoner to decide whether abortion, pornography, etc. are moral, personal, or social-conventional issues. Once this is done, judgments and justifications are predictable. This was a major conclusion of Smetana's (1981) investigation of women's real-life decisions regarding abortion. Within this framework, group differences, such as those studied here, lie not in the cognitive structures of reasoning within domains (moral, social conventional, personal) but in the processes by which events are categorized into domains. This, in turn, raises the question of what determines how the issue is categorized.

[1] The other day, a group of friends, my wife, and I were discussing abortion. One friend, who is a clinical psychologist, a believing Protestant Christian, and an extremely thoughtful and responsible individual, said that she felt divided on the issue of abortion, opposing it on strictly ethical or philosophical (read deontological) grounds but supporting it on practical (read utilitarian) grounds. Her resolution is to favor abortion as a citizen and professional, but she indicated that she has some private misgivings about it because she is convinced that it is murder.

[2] Of course, this is an analogy of form, not a similarity of content. The nonprototypical issues under consideration here are extremely important for people and for society and not in any way to be reduced to the strictly cognitive issues in Piaget's tasks.

Nonprototypical events might be basically of two types. The first, which might be termed "ambiguous," is nonprototypical because of uncertainty as to whether the event involves issues of morality (the welfare of or fairness to others), or of social convention (the functioning of the group or society), or of the personal domain (the individuality and integrity of the person involved). The second, termed "complex," is not uncertain but rather compound in that it clearly involves elements or characteristics of more than one of the domains. Complex issues include those that elsewhere Smetana (1983) has termed "second-order events." For example, where uniformity serves as the basis of group harmony, breech of convention may involve harm to others; even more common are situations in which maintenance and functioning of the group (appear to) require actions that involve sacrifice of the individual's well-being or of the principle of fairness.

Two explanations seem plausible. One involves what might be termed a subordinate process, while the other involves a supraordinate structure. Ambiguity leads to explanation 4 (see below), which involves social cognitive processes, while complexity leads to 5 and issues of the interrelations of the domains themselves, that is, their organization or structure.

4. This explanation, which Turiel et al. term "relational determination" (after Asch, 1952), involves what are usually designated as social cognitive processes, such as causal attribution, and includes inferences as to the actor's intentions (as in studies of the child's conception of mind). According to this view, reasoning on nonprototypical issues depends on and derives from the reasoner's understanding and interpretation of the situation, what Turiel et al. call "social construals." For example, what might make abortion such a difficult and divisive issue is that people differ in their belief as to when life begins, which is a pseudo-empirical, not a strictly moral, issue. Once the decision is made as to when life begins, the issue is treated either as moral or as personal, and judgments and justifications follow accordingly. This is the point of view that the authors seem to favor in their general discussion, and it was also a central point in Turiel, Killen, and Helwig's (1987) critique of Shweder's (1986) position.

5. Finally, the categorization of complex nonprototypical issues might be problematic because reasoners have different supraordinate structures within which morality, social convention, personal domains, etc. are placed. That is, when particular acts share characteristics of more than one of the basic domains, the question becomes which judgments and justifications take precedence. These structures might themselves be based on some fundamental beliefs about the relation between the individual and society (see the discussion below). There are a number of ways of resolving conflicts that arise from such overlap of domains. One domain might take precedence or dominate the other, or features of two or more domains might be combined,

or a new (ad hoc?) structure might be formed to deal with this nonprototypical or special case.

These five constitute neither a definitive nor a mutually exclusive list of explanations of nonprototypicality, but they do include those raised by Turiel and his colleagues plus others that seem reasonable to me. The first three concern the nature of nonprototypical issues themselves, while the last two concern still more fundamental issues of how morality and other belief systems articulate with other cognitive systems and processes. Let us now consider these formulations in the light of a selective examination of the empirical findings reported in the *Monograph*.

The Research Findings

In the first study, high school and college students were preselected on their (surface) opinion about one of four nonprototypical issues: abortion, pornography, homosexuality, and incest (each subject was presented with only one of these). Their judgments and reasoning were then compared to their thinking on two of three moral issues (killing, rape, and theft) and on one of three personal issues (nudity at a public beach, smoking marijuana, and men wearing makeup). Two groups were formed. The first consisted of those who evaluated the nonprototypical issue negatively and the second of those who evaluated it positively. The purpose of the design was to determine how opposite stances on nonprototypical issues related to the reasoners' judgments and reasoning on the prototypical (moral and personal) issues.

The basic finding was that, although the two groups differed clearly in their position on the generalizability and contingency of the nonprototypical issues (not unexpectedly, given that they had been selected to contrast evaluative stances on these issues), they did not differ in their judgments of either moral or personal prototypical issues. That is, reasoners in Group 1 condemned abortion etc., but most thought that it should be legal in the United States, although it was wrong even if legal or commonly practiced; those in Group 2 approved of abortion etc. and uniformly thought not only that it should be legal but also that it was right even if illegal or uncommonly practiced. However, despite such marked differences in this regard, the two groups did not differ in their comparable responses to questions concerning moral issues (killing, rape; see Tables 5 and 6). Nor did they differ in their views about issues squarely in the personal domain, believing them to be nongeneralizable and contingent on law or custom. Thus, their judgments on nonprototypical issues could not be predicted from their judgments or reasoning (see the justifications listed in Table 10) in the prototypical moral domain.

The overall pattern of results, both in this *Monograph* and in Turiel and his colleagues' previous studies, does not support explanation 1 in that the reasoning used in dealing with the nonprototypical issues does not parallel that used in reasoning about the moral issues. Can the pattern of results be explained as a décalage in thought (as in explanation 2 above)?[3] What tends to cast doubt on this explanation is that few age differences are evident in the log-linear analyses (Table 7). The only such that emerged involves the degree to which evaluative judgments depend on legal status in the United States, with high school students exhibiting this dependency more than college students. This offers at best very limited support for the décalage interpretation of the findings. In addition, past results reported by Turiel and his colleagues and students (e.g., Turiel, 1983) also fail to support this kind of explanation, although it should be noted that a wider age or developmental range would have provided a better test of this hypothesis.

Is it then possible that the groups differ because of differences in the categorization of the nonprototypical? That is, does the difference depend on how each categorizes or labels the issues, with Group 2 categorizing them as personal, while Group 1 does not? There is some support for this explanation. As the authors note, "Some claim that abortion is killing, whereas others assert that it affects none other than the woman making the decision" (p. 76). Groups 1 and 2 do differ in their judgments of strictly personal issues (Table 9), but this is only a partial explanation since the parallel between judgment patterns given for the personal and the nonprototypical holds only for Group 2, not for Group 1. Thus, Group 2 might be "partial libertarians," although certainly not in the moral domain; also, the reasons/justifications given for issues in the personal domain (Table 11) are not very different between the two groups. Nonetheless, it is possible that Group 2 members assimilate nonprototypical issues to the personal domain. But then who are those in Group 1? Their general orientation is very different from that of Group 2 (see Table 14) in that they frequently use combinations of moral, normative, or consequential reasons along with personal reasons (wrong but should not be prohibited), whereas those in Group 2 rely on personal orientations in judging these nonprototypical issues. Also, even if it were established that these two groups categorize the issues differently, the question still remains whether the categorization is the critical mediating event or whether it is rather a by-product of fundamentally different processes.

Perhaps Turiel et al. reasoned that selecting a more ideologically or religiously committed group would shed light on what is going on, especially

[3] Findings consistent with an explanation in terms of décalage would show parallel developmental differences (e.g., changes with chronological or mental age), but the rate of growth would be greater for nonprototypical than for prototypical judgments.

109

in Group 1. Accordingly, they selected a group of religiously committed students attending Roman Catholic parochial schools who, they assumed, would match the results obtained for Group 1 in Study 1. However, the same diversity of opinions was found in this sample, revealing subsamples that again differed on these nonprototypical issues but not on the moral ones and confirming the findings from Study 1 and its less selective group of students. Thus, religious affiliation and group commitment do not seem to explain positions taken on the nonprototypical issues, at least not for the majority of the subjects.

This brings us to explanation 4, that differences in judgment and reasoning on these nonprototypical issues depend on how the issue is categorized, which in turn depends on the reasoners' assumptions about and analysis of the situation. In this view, the difference between the pro- and antiabortion groups rests on whether they believe that life begins at birth, or at conception, or somewhere during gestation; similarly, the difference between those tolerant and intolerant of homosexuality rests and is determined by their conception of what is normal sexuality. Turiel et al. did find a relation between these beliefs (social construals) and concomitant judgments—more clearly for abortion than for homosexuality—but through a series of conditional probes demonstrate quite convincingly, in my view, that *these* differences in social construals do not solely account for the divisive differences in judgments. For example, when they asked those who favored abortion and believed that life begins at birth whether abortion was an appropriate means of selecting sex, most demurred. This is a very important observation in that it strongly suggests that there is more to one's position on abortion than the quasi-empirical question of when life begins. Further, it suggests that moral reasoners may not fully know themselves why they oppose or are in favor of abortion rights. (It is also noteworthy that the two examples given involve what might be termed "quasi-empirical" issues since they probably cannot be resolved by empirical evidence.)

Before going on, however, let me emphasize that I strongly agree with Turiel et al. that social construals—that is, assumptions about and interpretations of the situation—are critical in understanding developmental and other group differences in moral judgment. So, for example, in my own research on moral intentionality (e.g., Saltzstein, 1987; Saltzstein & Atwell, 1991), the working hypothesis is that causal reasoning is what determines, or at least strongly influences, how and when intentionality is used as a criterion in moral judgment. Whether or not this particular hypothesis is correct, in my judgment the question of whether social construals account for individual and group differences is crucial for understanding moral cognitive development. In the present context, the social construal explanation might best account for judgment and reasoning when the issue is ambiguous as to its appropriate categorization. But what about situations where it is not ambiguity but complexity that is the source of the difficulty, that is, where there is no ambiguity as to which domain (category) the issue belongs to but where it is rather that the issue unambiguously belongs to more than one domain?

This brings us to the fifth explanation, namely, that differences in reasoning patterns about nonprototypical issues reflect supraordinate differences in the assumed and perhaps also implicit beliefs about how these domains are related to one another. This is suggested by respondents who argue that, while they are morally wrong, abortion etc. are not properly under the jurisdiction of society. The philosopher Dworkin, I think, implies the same in his discussion of abortion in the *New York Review of Books* (1989). Dworkin suggests that the critical issue is not when life begins but what kind of life is (should be?) constitutionally protected. In this framework, the issue is converted from a pseudo-empirical or scientific one to a bona fide social-political issue and ultimately to how to conceive of the relation between the individual and society. It may then be that this and other such disagreements *within* the society are what differentiate Groups 1 and 2.

The resolution of these issues influences the way in which the various domains are organized, and that becomes evident only or primarily when complex or compound nonprototypical issues, that is, those that share components of two or more domains, are judged. Such issues are not rare. They serve as one of the main sources of social conflict in people's decisions and are often the central issue in dramas featuring social-moral dilemmas.

The question then becomes what fundamental principles might serve as overarching principles for these evaluative systems. Let me suggest some, a list that should be taken to be neither exhaustive nor definitive. The first two are based on Durkheim's (1984/1933) classic discussion of the division of labor in society. They are solidarity with others based on similarity (homogeneity or what Durkheim called "mechanical solidarity") and solidarity based on differentiation and interdependence ("organic solidarity"). Social convention may be related to Durkheim's mechanical solidarity in that uniformity of beliefs (although not necessarily of action) is believed to promote the solidarity of the group. Mechanical solidarity may, of course, involve differentiations of role and status. However, it is based on deference to and respect for the group, which is the subjective basis of social convention. Organic solidarity, that is, solidarity based on interdependence of roles, seems to me to be more closely connected to morality (see Piaget, 1932) in that this kind of solidarity rests on twin moral principles: the utilitarian one of concern for consequences for others and the deontological principle of fairness/justice resting on what Rawls and others have termed the "veil" position, that roles (perspectives) are impersonal rather than personal and may be adopted by anyone to whom the rights and responsibilities then apply.

Other possibly relevant factors have to do with how the individual relates to the larger society: directly, as individual to society, or through mediated connections via lower-level social groupings (family, clan, etc.). (This is analogous to the ways in which different religions, e.g., Catholicism, evangelical Protestantism, Judaism, etc., conceive of the relationship between the individual and God.) This belief itself may be further related to the assumption that society is established and continually reestablished by a contract among individuals or that society exists prior to the individual and receives the individual into its body. Other possible underlying principles have to do with the implicit assumptions about whether society should serve solely as a limit on the activities of individuals (i.e., to prevent Hobbes's feared war of all against all) or also to promote the well-being of the individual, an issue that divides political liberals and conservatives.

Whether these particular ideas eventually prove useful remains an open question. The main point is that these or other principles of similar kinds need to be explored to see whether they can account for how the moral, conventional, personal, etc. belief systems are organized. It is this organization of belief systems that I am suggesting influences how the domains are coordinated when complex or compound situations have to be judged (e.g., Turiel & Smetana, 1984; Turiel et al., 1987). Further, we should consider these overarching principles, not as characterizing whole cultures for reasons argued by Turiel, Smetana, and Killen (in press), but as principles underlying all societies and by which societies differ by their emphasis.

Thus, on this view, it is the very place of morality in social relations that determines what happens when a nonprototypical issue whose nonprototypicality does not rest or rest solely on the interpretation or construal of the situation (as in explanation 4 above) is encountered. This means that moral development is not driven solely bottom up by the development of its components, notably perspective taking and causal attribution (as assumed in classic cognitive-structural and social psychological theory), but also top down by an overall conceptualization of the organization of moral, conventional, personal, and other aspects of social life. I began this Commentary by suggesting that the work done here and before by Turiel and his coworkers shows how a field of inquiry develops by a series of differentiations in keeping with Werner's (1948) orthogenic principle. What I am suggesting now is that, consistent with the same principle, there is a need for showing how the domains themselves must be integrated at higher (supraordinate) conceptual levels. Questions remain concerning whether the organization of these domains is itself subject to developmental change, as a result of a growing implicit understanding of these (proposed) underlying principles.

Future Directions

Four next directions for research suggest themselves to me. The first two involve exploring the interactions among and the coordination of domains further by even more intensive interviewing. Such an approach might adopt two strategies. One would be to do more of the same, that is, to undertake still deeper and even more probing questioning along the lines of Study 3, such as, for example, asking the respondents to imagine themselves in different social contexts (e.g., a more or less homogeneous society) when asking for criterion judgments and justifications.

A second approach would be to use techniques similar to those of decision makers (e.g., Newell & Simon, 1972) to provide a better account of the *process* of social/moral decision making. This might require identifying less well-practiced variants of these social issues since familiar situations are not as likely to reveal the decision-making process in any detail. For example, the new birth-control (abortion?) drug developed in France, which provides a method of birth control by means of abortion very early in the pregnancy, might serve as such a new problem to "solve." To my knowledge, aside from Shultz's computational model (1987; Darley & Shultz, 1990; and Shultz & Schleifer, 1983), moral reasoning has not looked at the process of making moral judgments from a decision-making point of view, although lately some writers (e.g., Kurtines, 1984; Rest, 1983) have suggested sequential formulations that might be rendered as decision structures. The advantage of such an approach is twofold. First, it enables us to connect the study of morality with the large and rich body of decision making (e.g., Hogarth, 1980); second, as I have argued elsewhere (Saltzstein, 1991), the conceptualization of moral reasoning in decision-making terms may provide a common theoretical framework for connecting moral thought and action.

A third research strategy would lie in devising influence interventions to determine whether different kinds of interventions are differentially effective in changing judgments. This strategy follows Lewin's (1951) suggestion that one way to understand a phenomenon is to try to change it. If judgments of nonprototypical issues are not based on moral criteria but are (partly) based on considerations in the personal domains, influence techniques that appeal to welfare and fairness concerns should not be effective in inducing change in judgment, but appeals based on personal autonomy should be. This would be an extension of what Turiel et al. did in their probes in the third study.

A fourth approach would be to compare the results of these empirical (synthetic) studies with results of philosophical (analytic) studies (e.g., Cohen, Nagel, & Scanlon, 1974). For example, in her chained-violinist argument, Thomson (1975) has shown how one might disapprove of abortion in the general case but not in the special cases of rape and incest (a position I had always thought self-contradictory).[4] Thomson accomplishes this, I think, by distinguishing between (perfect) duties to do good and nonobligatory (imperfect) duties. Do everyday reasoners about abortion understand and use this distinction implicitly in making their own judgments? In general, opinion polls show clearly that judgments of abortion are not based simply on the belief about when life begins since the phrasing of the question and the context in which it is presented very much determine the distribution of opinions.

In general, a next theoretical step would be to conceptualize the relation among three components: the social construals (interpretations and representations of the situation), the structures of the domains (moral, social conventional, personal, etc.), and the meta- or supradomain structures in which the fundamental relation between individual and society is represented.

Conclusion

In general, the strength of the work reported by Turiel et al. in this *Monograph* lies in its choice of issues (which are socially important and cognitively complex), its careful and intensive examination of the respondents' beliefs, and its discussion of these issues within the framework of a rich and sophisticated body of research and theory. It seems to me that the findings suggest how individual and group differences *cannot* be explained more than how they can. This is indeed extremely important because, by exploring the limits of moral theory, the *Monograph* suggests a need to place moral theory itself within a broader and deeper supraordinate context.

While the studies are not developmental in the superficial sense of the term, that is, they do not focus on age differences, they are very important for theories of moral and more generally social development in that they point to the fundamental organization of moral and social thought within which a developmental progression must operate. Further, they point the way to a still more top-down comprehensive approach to the development of social thought.

Adopting a broader and more functional perspective, I see this *Mono-*

[4] Thomson poses the following situation. A person awakes to find herself connected to an unconscious world-famous violinist. The violinist will die if they are disconnected because he has a rare blood disease and requires the use of this particular person's kidney for 9 months (or years . . .). Through an analysis of this unusual situation, Thomson shows how one can be against abortion in general but approve of it in cases of rape, incest, etc., that is, where the woman's consent was not given. The argument rests on the distinction between absolute duties (e.g., not to kill) and nonabsolute ones (e.g., to give charity), a distinction emphasized by Kant (1964/1785).

graph and much of Turiel's and his coworkers' research as serving to define morality and preserve its status as universal, rational, and absolute, a goal with which I am in sympathy.

Turiel and his coworkers have opened a rich area of psychological inquiry with ties to and implications for developmental and social psychology, sociology and anthropology, philosophy, and public policy. In this careful investigation of the edges of morality, they have revealed and explored fundamental questions about the nature of social and moral thought.

References

Aronfreed, J. (1968). *Conduct and conscience: The socialization of internalized control over behavior.* New York: Academic.

Asch, S. (1952). *Social psychology.* Englewood Cliffs, NJ: Prentice-Hall.

Bandura, A., & Walters, R. (1963). *Social learning and personality development.* New York: Holt, Rinehart & Winston.

Cohen, M., Nagel, T., & Scanlon, T. (1974). *The rights and wrongs of abortion.* Princeton, NJ: Princeton University Press.

Darley, J. M., & Shultz, T. R. (1990). Moral rules: Their content and acquisition. In M. R. Rosenzweig & L. W. Porter (Eds.), *Annual review of psychology* (Vol. **41**). Palo Alto, CA: Annual Reviews.

Durkheim, E. (1961). *Moral education.* Glencoe, Ill.: Free Press. (First published in 1925)

Durkheim, E. (1984). *The division of labor in society* (G. Simpson, Trans.). New York: Free Press. (Original work published in French in 1933)

Dworkin, R. (1989, July 29). The great abortion case. *New York Review of Books,* pp. 49–53.

Frankena, W. (1973). *Ethics.* Englewood Cliffs, NJ: Prentice-Hall.

Hogarth, R. M. (1980). *Judgment and choice: The psychology of decision making.* New York: Wiley.

Kant, I. (1964). *Groundwork of the metaphysics of morals* (H. J. Paton, Trans.). New York: Harper & Row. (Original work published in 1785)

Kurtines, W. M. (1984). Moral behavior as rule-governed behavior: A psychosocial role-theoretical approach to moral behavior and development. In W. M. Kurtines & J. R. Gewirtz (Eds.), *Morality, moral behavior, and moral development* (pp. 303–324). New York: Wiley.

Lewin, K. (1951). *Field theory in social psychology.* New York: Harper & Row.

Newell, A., & Simon, H. (1972). *Human problem-solving.* Englewood Cliffs, NJ: Prentice-Hall.

Piaget, J. (1932). *The moral judgement of the child.* London: Routledge & Kegan Paul.

Rawls, J. (1971). *A theory of justice.* Cambridge, Mass.: Harvard University Press.

Rest, J. (1983). Morality. In J. H. Flavell & E. M. Markman (Eds.), P. H. Mussen (Series Ed.), *Handbook of child psychology: Vol 3. Cognitive development* (pp. 556–629). New York: Wiley.

Saltzstein, H. D. (1987, April). The representation of other persons' moral judgments. In H. D. Saltzstein (Chair), *Moral responsibility and causal reasoning.* Symposium conducted at the annual meeting of the Society for Research in Child Development, Baltimore.

Saltzstein, H. D. (1991). *Comments on the relationship between moral thought and action.* Unpublished manuscript.

Saltzstein, H. D., & Atwell, J. (1991). *Difference between own and attributed moral judgments: Self-other or parent-child phenomenon?* Unpublished manuscript.

Searle, J. (1990, December 6). The battle over the university. *New York Review of Books,* pp. 34–42.

Shultz, T. R. (1987, April). A computational model of causation, responsibility, blame, and punishment. In H. D. Saltzstein (Chair), *Moral responsibility and causal reasoning.* Symposium conducted at the annual meeting of the Society for Research in Child Development, Baltimore.

Shultz, T. R., & Schleifer, M. (1983). Towards a refinement of attribution concepts. In J. Jaspars, F. D. Fincham, & M. Hewstone (Eds.), *Attribution theory and research: Conceptual, developmental and social dimensions* (pp. 37–62). London: Academic.

Shweder, R. A. (1986). Divergent rationalities. In D. W. Fiske & R. A. Shweder (Eds.), *Metatheory in social science: Pluralism and subjectivities* (pp. 163–196). Chicago: University of Chicago Press.

Shweder, R. A. (1990). In defense of moral realism. *Child Development,* **61,** 2060–2067.

Smetana, J. (1981). Reasoning in the personal and moral domains: Adolescent and young adult women's decision-making regarding abortion. *Journal of Applied Developmental Psychology,* **3,** 211–226.

Smetana, J. (1983). Social-cognitive development: Domain distinctions and coordinations. *Developmental Review,* **3,** 131–147.

Thomson, J. J. (1975). A defense of abortion: A compromise view. *Philosophy and Public Affairs,* **1,** 197–210.

Turiel, E. (1983). *The development of social knowledge: Morality and convention.* Cambridge: Cambridge University Press.

Turiel, E., Killen, M., & Helwig, C. C. (1987). Morality: Its structure, functions, and vagaries. In J. Kagan & S. Lamb (Eds.), *The emergence of morality in young children.* Chicago: University of Chicago Press.

Turiel, E., & Smetana, J. (1984). Social knowledge and action: The coordination of domains. In W. M. Kurtines & J. R. Gewirtz (Eds.), *Morality, moral behavior, and moral development* (pp. 261–282). New York: Wiley.

Turiel, E., Smetana, J., & Killen, M. (in press). Social contexts in social cognitive development. In W. M. Kurtines & J. L. Gewirtz (Eds.), *Handbook of moral behavior and development: Vol. 2. Research.* Hillsdale, NJ: Erlbaum.

Werner, H. (1948). *Comparative psychology of mental development.* New York: Science Editions.

CONTRIBUTORS

Elliot Turiel (Ph.D. 1965, Yale University) is professor of education and research psychologist in the Institute of Human Development at the University of California, Berkeley. His research interests are in moral and social cognitive development.

Carolyn Hildebrandt (Ph.D. 1985, University of California, Berkeley) is an assistant research psychologist in the Institute of Human Development at the University of California, Berkeley. Her research interests are in social cognitive development and children's musical comprehension.

Cecilia Wainryb (Ph.D. 1989, University of California, Berkeley) is a postdoctoral fellow in psychology at the University of Haifa. Her research interests are in moral and social cognitive development.

Herbert D. Saltzstein (Ph.D. 1962, University of Michigan) is professor of and executive officer of the doctoral program in psychology at the Graduate School and University Center of the City University of New York. His current research interests are in children's and adolescents' moral and social cognitive development, the relation between moral action and thought, and medical decision making.

STATEMENT OF EDITORIAL POLICY

The *Monographs* series is intended as an outlet for major reports of developmental research that generate authoritative new findings and use these to foster a fresh and/or better-integrated perspective on some conceptually significant issue or controversy. Submissions from programmatic research projects are particularly welcome; these may consist of individually or group-authored reports of findings from some single large-scale investigation or of a sequence of experiments centering on some particular question. Multiauthored sets of independent studies that center on the same underlying question can also be appropriate; a critical requirement in such instances is that the various authors address common issues and that the contribution arising from the set as a whole be both unique and substantial. In essence, irrespective of how it may be framed, any work that contributes significant data and/or extends developmental thinking will be taken under editorial consideration.

Submissions should contain a minimum of 80 manuscript pages (including tables and references); the upper limit of 150–175 pages is much more flexible (please submit four copies; a copy of every submission and associated correspondence is deposited eventually in the archives of the SRCD). Neither membership in the Society for Research in Child Development nor affiliation with the academic discipline of psychology are relevant; the significance of the work in extending developmental theory and in contributing new empirical information is by far the most crucial consideration. Because the aim of the series is not only to advance knowledge on specialized topics but also to enhance cross-fertilization among disciplines or subfields, it is important that the links between the specific issues under study and larger questions relating to developmental processes emerge as clearly to the general reader as to specialists on the given topic.

Potential authors who may be unsure whether the manuscript they are planning would make an appropriate submission are invited to draft an outline of what they propose and send it to the Editor for assessment.

This mechanism, as well as a more detailed description of all editorial policies, evaluation processes, and format requirements, is given in the "Guidelines for the Preparation of *Monographs* Submissions," which can be obtained by writing to Wanda C. Bronson, Institute of Human Development, 1203 Tolman Hall, University of California, Berkeley, CA 94720.